*ohio*

# MATTERS OF FACT

# MATTERS OF FACT

## By Damaine Vonada

ORANGE FRAZER PRESS
WILMINGTON, OHIO

Printed in the United States of America

Library of Congress Catalogue Card Number:
90-63038

Published by Orange Frazer Press, Inc.
P.O. Box 610
Wilmington, Ohio 45177

9.95

# Credits

---

Research assistants, *Jeff Plungis, Monica Vonada, Nathan Vonada*

Special thanks, *Sam Roshon,* Public Library of Columbus and Franklin County. *Dr. Michael C. Hansen,* Ohio Department of Natural Resources, Division of Geological Survey. Library of Congress, Prints and Photographs Division. McKinley Museum of History, Science, and Industry. Rutherford B. Hayes Presidential Center.

*Fred Nieman* and the National Park Service

Designer and illustrator, *Brooke Wenstrup*

Research consultant, *Dave Stephenson*

920828

# Table of contents

**The color of money**
How an Ohioan became our foremost
decorator
*page fifteen*

**False starts**
A list of obscure pre-occupations
*page sixteen*

**Catchwords**
A semantic sampling of Ohio originals
*page eighteen*

**Grand finales**
Last but never least
*page twenty*

**First**
Initial steps in matters great and small
*page twenty-four*

**None but the brave**
The first Congressional Medal of Honor
recipients
*page twenty-six*

**On the record**
Ohio measures up
*page thirty*

**Weather, or not**
Mean and magnificent moments
*page thirty-six*

*Honorable mentions*
Going far afield with the good names of Ohio
*page thirty-eight*

**One of a kind**
Items, oddities, and events found only in Ohio
*page forty-two*

**Down on the farm**
Ohio the bountiful, God bless her
*page forty-four*

*Inventory*
Our favorite Ohio inventions
*page forty-eight*

*National Standings*
Ohio vs. the other forty-nine — how we stack up
*page fifty-two*

**The essential Ohio bookshelf**
Several folks you should have over for dinner
*page fifty-four*

*Great appellations*
Nearby places with faraway names
*page fifty-eight*

*A Presidential album*
Native sons: Ohio presides over America
*page sixty-five*

**Landmark foods**
First in the stomachs of our countrymen
*page ninety-seven*

**Quotables from notables**
Ohioan spoken here
*page one hundred*

**Cheap shots**
Some insubstantial, below-the-belt remarks
*page one hundred two*

**Coronets**
Thanks for a warm hand on a cold morning
*page one hundred six*

**Itchy feet**
Giving in to wanderlust
*page one hundred eight*

**The annotated Ohio**
The lay of the land
*page one hundred twelve*

**Going native**
Tribal rites, signs, and ceremonies
*page one hundred fourteen*

**Intestinal fortitude**
Great moments in Buckeye gastronomy
*page one hundred twenty-two*

**Eat Ohio**
Food for thought
*page one hundred twenty-four*

**Sobriquets**
By their nicknames we shall know them
*page one hundred twenty-six*

**Ladies of the club**
Women of means, manner, and method
*page one hundred twenty-eight*

**Ohio geology**
A garden of our earthly delights
*page one hundred thirty-six*

**Those magnificent men**
A few brief shining moments in Dayton
*page one hundred forty*

**Natural wonders**
Standouts in any crowd
*page one hundred forty-six*

**The body politic**
The facts of Ohio's political life
*page one hundred fifty*

# Foreword

*The way to do research is to attack the facts at the point of greatest astonishment.*

— Celia Green

The state of Ohio is an unwieldy creature. Long on geographies, tall in history, broad in cultures. **Bull**-headed about politics and religion. Given **to frequent** displays of fierce contradiction. Well-known for a seemingly uncontrollable urge to stray from its own territory and water the neighbors' shrubbery with all manner of deeds and intentions, genius and folly, inventions and ideas. But what a grand and glorious beast is Ohio — Heartland of a Nation, Mother of Presidents, Wet Nurse to the Air Age, Grand Central Station of the Underground Railroad, and Home Sweet Home to the quintessentially American Wright Brothers, Annie Oakley, Jeep, cash register, and Toledo scale.

Trying to put Ohio in perspective puts us in a postition rather like the fabled blind men of Hindustan — how we define the mammoth depends largely on where we stand and how far we can reach. In order for folks to truly appreciate this grand and complex state, we prefer to handle the beast by just roping it in a bit. Oh, we want a firm grip on Ohio, all right, but we see information as a tether rather than a noose. Used imaginatively, facts and figures can organize, manage, define, and reveal. We have tried to control Ohio by putting it on a long leash, lending it as broad a berth editorially as the state has enjoyed socially, economically, and historically. We want Ohio to be a *lively* exhibit. Interesting. Intriguing. Unpredictable. Full of nuance, surprises, and texture. A place worth celebrating and certainly worth reading about.

*Ohio Matters of Fact* is a multi-level, multi-dimensional approach to defining the state. Part list, part compendium, part essay, part reportage, it not only presents familiar kinds of information in unfamiliar ways, but also offers uncommon information by providing the kind of arcane but telling details that other reference works tend to overlook. Quite simply, *Ohio Matters of Fact* is a perspective, Ohio as a mindset, or at least how Ohio exists in the mind's eye, which in our case is wont to see the quirky, the offbeat, the whimsical. Our volume is admittedly a little, well, cockeyed. Traditional references usually approach information through the front door; we're likely to go in the back, down the chimney, maybe even through the cellar to seek out information that readers may not easily find elsewhere. Our ambition in *Ohio Matters of Fact* is that hoary goal of informing as well as entertaining. While we want this volume to be an Ohio resource, we humbly hope that it will prove to be a truly readable one as well.

Of course, we make no claim that *Ohio Matters of Fact* is the last word on this extraordinary state. We believe, in fact, that the last word lies in the hearts and minds of every Ohioan, and therefore, we invite readers to enlighten us by writing to P.O. Box 31101, Dayton, Ohio 45431. We welcome your information, anecdotes, objections, and, most certainly, your facts.

Damaine Vonada

Dayton, Ohio
July, 1987

# The color of money

## How an Ohioan became the country's foremost decorator

Green, said **Salmon P. Chase,** make it green, and so the color of U.S. paper currency was forever determined by a former Governor of Ohio.

During the Civil War when Chase served as Lincoln's Secretary of the Treasury, he established the national banking system and issued the federal government's first paper money good for legal tender. Union soldiers paid with the new paper dollars dubbed them "greenbacks," which, given the American penchant for slang, in turn led to "lettuce" and "cabbage" as synonymns for money.

It was Chase, by the way, who also gave us "In God We Trust." Many citizens felt that the dire circumstances of Civil War required some public appeal to a Higher Authority, and Chase obliged them by putting those four words on a 2-cent coin in 1864. In 1955, Congress mandated that they appear on all U.S. money, and the next year, "In God We Trust" replaced "E Pluribus Unum" ("from many, one" in Latin) as the nation's official motto. Ptolemy I of Egypt was the first to put an imperial visage (his own) on a coin, and nations have been putting portraits of their leaders on money ever since. Ohioans of banknote are

| | |
|---|---|
| *Ulysses S. Grant* | $50 bill |
| *William McKinley* | $500 |
| *Salmon P. Chase* | $10,000 |

Ironically, the $10,000 bill with Chase's portrait is the highest denomination of U.S. paper money still in circulation since the Treasury's 1969 decision to put a $100 cap on currency issued. Of the ten thousand Chase bills printed in 1944, about 340 are still held by private parties and have yet to revert to the Treasury.

# False starts

## A list of obscure pre-occupations

Milan-born *Thomas Edison* — night shift telegraph operator

Darke County broadcasting legend *Lowell Thomas* — gold miner

Entertainer *Dean Martin* — pumped gasoline in Steubenville

*Margaret Hamilton,* the Wicked Witch in *The Wizard of Oz* — manager of a Cleveland nursery school

Lancaster native *General William Tecumseh Sherman* — banker

Preeminent Dayton poet **Paul Laurence Dunbar** — elevator operator

Writer *Sherwood Anderson* — paint factory manager in Clyde

Legendary New York newspaper columnist *O. O. McIntyre* — Gallipolis hotel clerk

Airplane inventors *Wilbur and Orville Wright* — Dayton bicycle builders and salesmen

Celebrated Ross County folk artist *Tella Kitchen* — premier Model-T salesperson in Adelphi

Hollywood movie king *Clark Gable* — $95-a-month clerk at Firestone, Akron

Abolitionist *John Brown* — shepherd in Akron

*Birds of America* painter *John James Audubon* — Cincinnati taxidermist

Movie moguls, Youngstown's own **Warner Brothers** — Albert, soap saleman; Harry, meat salesman; Sam, carnival barker; Jack, deliveryman

**Zane Grey** sold off his office equipment to finance his first novel, an act of considerable self-confidence for a dentist from Zanesville. His gamble was *Betty Zane,* the story of a pioneer ancestor who singlehandedly saved an Ohio River fort and married the man who cut the first government road — Zane's Trace — through the wilderness of the Northwest Territory. But then, with material like that in one's family tree, who needs bridgework? Certainly not Grey, the "Father of the Adult Western" whose books — among them the popular *Riders of the Purple Sage* — have sold more than 130,000,000 copies.

# Catchwords

### *"Automobile"*

The word, which certainly has a better ring than horseless carriage, was supposedly coined circa 1897 by a reporter for the Cleveland *Plain Dealer* when local manufacturer **Alexander Winton** gave him a ride.

### *"Bionics"*

In the 1960's, the Bio-Engineering Laboratory at Wright-Patterson Air Force Base, Dayton, came up with this term for applying biological system solutions to technical problems.

### *"Bogus"*

A Lake County newspaper, the *Painesville Telegraph*, originated this adjective in 1827 when some locals went on trial for counterfeiting silver dollars. The paper described their equipment as "bogus," and within two decades, the word was part of the nation's vocabulary. By the way, the defendants were acquitted because the jury decided that the poor quality dollars were so blatently bogus they couldn't possibly fool anybody.

### *"Buck"*

The word became a slang synonym for a dollar because hunters on the Ohio frontier sold hides of male deer — buckskins — for a dollar each.

### *"Get Down to Brass Tacks"*

According to an apocryphal story, this phrase originated in Ohio's general stores, where cloth lengths were measured by brass tacks set at intervals in a counter.

### *"Mend Some Fences"*

This metaphor has been attributed to **John Sherman,** Ohio Senator and Secretary of the Treasury.

### "Land Office Business"

After William Henry Harrison helped persuade Congress to open the Northwest Territory to the public, the Harrison Land Act of 1800 allowed settlers to purchase tracts of land at reasonable rates and terms. In three years, more than a million acres were sold, and by 1820, a flood of settlers was swamping fourteen land offices north of the Ohio River.

### "Rock 'n' Roll"

In 1951, *Alan Freed,* a disc jockey at WJW in Cleveland, was the first to broadcast this Black idiom.

### "Spring Ahead and Fall Back"

*Gordon Rawlinson,* a Westlake schoolteacher, claims he invented this maxim in the 1960's to give his students a helping hand through the complexities of daylight savings time.

### "Yellow Journalism"

In October, 1897, Lancaster native *Richard Outcault* began drawing "The Yellow Kid" for Joseph Pulitzer's *New York World.* It was the first color comic strip, and Outcalt's title got applied to slipshod reporting when Pulitzer and William Randolph Hearst started slinging sensationalism in a circulation war.

### "Zipper"

Originally, zippers weren't fasteners, but galoshes manufactured by the B.F. Goodrich Company of Akron in the early 1920's. But folks got their Zipper Boots confused with the gadget that held them on their feet, and "hookless fasteners" have been called zippers ever since.

# Grand finales

Faded away — ***John Gray,*** last surviving soldier of the American Revolution, died Hiramsburg, Ohio, March 29, 1868, age 104 ♥

Convention suspension — for Cincinnati, which saw its latest political party conclave in 1876; the Republicans came to town to nominate Ohio's favorite son ***Rutherford Hayes*** for President

Peaked streak — the decade-long, 122-meet winning record of Dayton runner par excellance ***Edwin Moses*** ended June 4, 1987; bested in the 400 meter hurdles by Danny Harris

Final farm in Cleveland — ***Neil Richardson's*** 5.5 acres spread near the Cuyahoga River

Mule pull — ended in the U.S. May 4, 1918, when the last equine-powered car line, Middletown Street Car Railway, ceased service

Shaker quaker — last Shaker gristmill in Ohio dynamited July 4, 1886, in Cleveland

The last voice in the wilderness — Gallia County native ***Orval L. Hall,*** the Methodist Church's last circuit riding minister, died February 5, 1977, in Columbus

Bye, Bye, ***"Blackbird"*** — last operational SR-71 spy plane, Air Force Museum, Dayton

Curtain call — the ***Showboat Majestic,*** Cincinnati, is the last of the original riverboat theaters still afloat

Tobacco road — for Belmont's ***Harley Warrick,*** last working Mail Pouch sign painter

Milk stop — West Lafayette, home of Coshocton Valley Manufacturing Co., last milk can maker in North America

Ends of the earth — a small Miami tract between the St. Marys River and the Greenville Treaty line was the last non-reserve Ohio Indian land ceded to the U.S., Oct. 6, 1818

Sarah Bernhardt swan song — the actress's farewell U.S. performance was 1918 in Cleveland; the play, *Arriere Les Huns;* the place, Keith's Hippodrome

Bitter end — **Martha,** only remaining member of the species *Ectopistes migratorius*, commonly called the passenger pigeon, died September 1, 1914, at the Cincinnati Zoo ♥

♥ Born at Mount Vernon, **John Gray** served George Washington well in many fields, both farm and battle. Present at Yorktown when General Cornwallis surrendered, Gray was mustered out of the Continental Army one day and back at work on Washington land the next. Gray came to Ohio before it was a state and hired out as a farm laborer. His Noble County neighbors knew him as a kindly man, dedicated to the Methodist church, dogs, and chewing tobacco. He lived long enough to witness yet another rebellion and the attendant cries for freedom. But even with the country preoccupied with Reconstruction, Congress granted him a $500-a- year pension. His epitaph tells why: *John Gray, the Last of Washington's Companions. The Hoary Head is a Crown of Glory.*

♥ **Martha** was born free, but died in captivity, albeit a benign one at the Cincinnati Zoological Gardens. Her heritage was rich and powerful, for she belonged to one of the most populous societies ever to grace the earth. The passenger pigeons' astronomical number (John James Audubon estimated that just *one* flock along the Ohio River had 1,115,000,000 members) was the stuff of their survival, for they were preeminently companionable creatures. "The pigeon was no mere bird," said naturalist Aldo Leopold, "he was a biological storm. He was the lightning that played between two biotic poles of intolerable intensity: the fat of the land and his own zest for living."

Like the prairie, the buffalo, and the forest, passenger pigeons seemed another of North America's inexhaustible resources, and so man hunted them mercilessly for food, for sport, for profit, for shame. In April, 1861, hunters at Circleville slaughtered 200,000 a day, sending their grim bonanza to cities like Cincinnati where a dozen birds brought fifty cents to a dollar. "Like any other chain-reaction, the pigeon could survive no diminution of his own furious intensity," noted Leopold. "Once the pigeoners had subtracted from his numbers, and once the settler had chopped gaps in the continuity of his fuel, his flame guttered out with hardly a sputter or even a wisp of smoke."

Little more than a hundred years after Audubon's spectacular sighting, Martha was the last passenger pigeon left on the planet. For fifteen years, the Cincinnati Zoo had a standing thousand dollar offer for a mate for Martha, but none was ever found. When she succumbed at 1 p.m. that first of September, her passing marked the first time that mankind could *document* the extinction of a species.

# First

## Initial steps in matters great and small

U.S. shot fired in World War I — by Cincinnati's Robert Braley of the American Expeditionary Forces

Air conditioned department store — F. R. Lazarus Company, Columbus, 1934

Train robbery — at North Bend, May 5, 1865 ♥

Dancing school chain — started by W. J. Rader, Columbus, 1898

Gasoline filling station — opened June 6, 1912, at the corner of Oak and Young, Columbus

U.S.-Indian tribe treaty — Signed by White Eyes of the Delaware, who was from what is now Muskingum County

Longhorn cattle west of the Platte River — taken by Athens native Nelson Story, Powder River cattle drive, 1866

Oil well — near South Olive, Noble County, 1814

Pet airline — operated by Richard Burns, Cincinnati, 1976

VFW post — Columbus, 1899

Concrete skyscraper — Ingalls Building, Fourth and Vine, Cincinnati, 1902

Disposable diaper — Pampers, from Procter & Gamble, Cincinnati, 1962

Electric traffic signals — at Euclid Ave. and E. 105th St., Cleveland, August 5, 1914

Foam-soled slipper — by R. G. Barry Company, Columbus, 1947

Gorilla born in captivity — Columbus Zoo, December 22, 1956

Nuclear reactor liability policy — written by McElroy Minster Company, Columbus

Radio broadcasting station — National Bank Building, Toledo, Dr. Lee DeForest and Frank Butler, 1907

Concrete street — Bellefontaine, 1891

Mile-a-minute automobile speed — Wauseon native Berna Eli "Barney" Oldfield, 1903

Crop dusting — Troy, an Army training plane dumped insecticide over worm-infested fields, 1920's


♥ The *Ohio and Mississippi train* was only fourteen miles from its Cincinnati destination when something blocked the rails, and the locomotive and baggage-and-express car overturned. Immediately, robbers appeared and set upon the train. They pilfered securities from the safe and relieved gentlemen passengers of their wallets. But even as the hooligans pulled off the first train robbery in the United States, they were not without their manners, for the ladies on board were excused from their larceny. The deed done, the robbers were reportedly seen on the Ohio River in rowboats, heading swiftly for the sanctuary of Kentucky.

# None but the brave

## The first Congressional Medal of Honor recipients

1. *Pvt. Jacob Parrott,* Fairfield County

2. *Pvt. William Bensinger,* Wayne County

3. *Pvt. Robert Buffum,* home unknown

4. *Sgt. Elihu H. Mason,* Wood County

5. *Sgt. William Pittenger,* Jefferson County

6. *Cpl. William H. Reddick,* home unknown

7. *Pvt. Samuel Slavens,* Pike County

8. *Cpl. Daniel A. Dorsey,* Fairfield County

9. *Pvt. Wilson W. Brown,* Logan County

10. *Cpl. Martin J. Hawkins,* Scioto County

11. *Pvt. William J. Knight,* Defiance County

12. *Pvt. John R. Porter,* Hancock County

13. *Pvt. Samuel Robertson,* Muskingum County

14. *Sgt. Major Marion A. Ross,* Champaign County

15. *Pvt. John A. Wilson,* Wood County

16. *Pvt. Mark Wood,* Portage County

❤ Given for acts of "conspicuous gallantry and intrepidity" which are "above and beyond the call of duty", the Congressional Medal of Honor is the nation's supreme award for military bravery. The first Americans given the Medal were Ohioans, the volunteers for what one Southern newspaper called "the deepest scheme that ever emanated from the brains of the Yankees" — the **Great Locomotive Chase** of the Civil War.

In April, 1862, Ohio soldiers helped Union spy James Andrews steal a Georgia train out from under the noses of the conductor and crew, who were taking a coffee break in a hotel near Atlanta. As Andrews and his party headed north toward Chattanooga in the *General*, they lacerated critical Confederate supply lines by pulling up track and wreaking destruction. The chagrined conductor gave chase on foot and by hand car until he persuaded the engineer of a southbound freight to disconnect his locomotive and take after the Yankees going backwards. With the *Texas* bearing down on them, the Ohio volunteers couldn't refuel wood and water, so they ran out of luck when the *General* literally ran out of steam — about ninety miles after the chase began. Arrested and tried as spies, some of the Ohioans were hanged. Others escaped. The rest were imprisoned.

Soon after the Medal of Honor was created in 1863, Congress recognized the train wreckers' derring-do and bestowed the first ones on March 25, 1863, to Parrott, Bensinger, Buffam, Mason, Pittinger, and Reddick, who were followed within the year by the other Andrews Raiders listed here.

♥ Ohio also sired the first of only eighteen Americans who have received the Medal *twice* — **Capt. Thomas Ward Custer,** New Rumley native, Union soldier, and brother of the more famous George Armstrong Custer. The first time, he rode into Confederate fire and singlehandedly captured an enemy standard and fourteen rebels at Namozine Church, Virginia, in 1863. The second time, he had two horses shot out from under him while capturing two Confederate flags, which he ceremoniously presented to his commanding officer, who was none other than his brother, George. While earning his second Medal at Sailor Creek, Virginia, in 1865, the doughty Capt. Custer was shot through the head, the bullet penetrating his right cheek and exiting behind the ear. George ordered him off the battlefield twice, and twice he refused to obey. Finally, Tom had to be arrested and forcibly taken to a hospital where his cruel wound was treated. Tom cheated death long enough to serve under his brother eleven years later at the Battle of the Little Big Horn, which is known as Custer's Last Stand, but which is more accurately Custers' Last Stand, for three Custer brothers — George, Tom, and Boston — perished there at the hands of the Cheyenne and Sioux.

Ohio's latest Medal of Honor recipients: Vietnam

1. *LCpl. Joe C. Paul,* Dayton, 1965

2. *Sgt. Donald Russell Long,* Blackfork, 1966

3. *Sgt. Sammy L. Davis,* Dayton, 1967

4. *PFC. Douglas E. Dickey,* Greenville, 1967

5. *Capt. Michael J. Estocin,* Akron, 1967

6. *Sgt. Charles Clinton Fleek,* Cincinnati, 1967

7. *PFC. Melvin Earl Newlin,* Wellsville, 1967

8. *Sp4c. Frank A. Herda,* Cleveland, 1968

9. *Sp4c. Joseph G. LaPointe, Jr.,* Dayton, 1969

10. *Sp4c. Gordon R. Roberts,* Middletown, 1969

11. *PFC. David F. Winder,* Columbus, 1970

12. *Lt. Brian Miles Thacker,* Columbus, 1971

The Ohioans recognized for their service in Vietnam ranged in age only from 18 (1) to 35 (1). Soldiers Dickey, Estocin, Fleek, LaPointe, Long, Newlin, Paul, and Winder received the award posthumously.

Of particular courage were Pfc. Dickey, Sgt. Fleek, Sp4c. Herda, and Sgt. Long, who imperiled themselves to save others by throwing themselves on hand grenades.

920828

# On the record

*Ohio measures up*

### Largest

Airship roster (passengers/crew) — 207 aboard *U.S. Akron*, 1931

Amish population — approximately 35,000, primarily in Wayne, Holmes, Stark, Tuscarawas, Geauga and Defiance Counties

Antique sweeper collection — Hoover Historical Center, North Canton

Exotic animal gamete bank — Center for Reproduction and Endangered Wildlife, Cincinnati

Bowling Tournament — Hoinke Classic, Western Bowl, Cincinnati

Males-only gardening club — Akron's Men's Garden Club, 300-plus members

Cuckoo clock — 26 by 23.5 feet, Alpine-Alpa Cheese Factory, Wilmot

Horticultural service company — Davey Tree Co., Kent; some 4000 employees and $150 million in annual sales

Database (on-line, full-text) — 92.7 million entries, Mead Data Central Lexis/Nexis, Dayton

Bell and carillon manufacturer — The Verdin Co., Cincinnati

Hangar — Loral Airdock, Akron; 1175 feet long; 325 feet wide, 211 feet high, 55 million cubic feet of space

Mason Grand Jurisdiction — 190,000 members in 656 lodges of the Grand Lodge of Free and Accepted Masons of Ohio

Eastern Star Grand Chapter memberships — 113,870 in Ohio's 500 chapters

Open geodesic dome — 274 feet diameter, Russell Township

Shoe lace manufacturer — Mitchellace, Portsmouth

Soap manufacturer — Procter & Gamble, Cincinnati

*Isotelus maximus* (trilobite) fossil — sixteen-by-ten-and-a-half-inches, found by Tom Johnson in Montgomery County, 1988

Twins convention — 1181 sets, Twinsburg, August, 1985

Horse show, single breed — American Quarter Horse Congress, Columbus

Public collection of Lotusware — Museum of Ceramics, East Liverpool

Lawn mower — sixty feet wide Big Green Machine, owned by Jay Edgar Frick, Monroe; mows one acre per minute

*McGuffey Reader* collection — Miami University, Oxford

Air fair and aviation trade exposition — the United States Air and Trade Show, Dayton, 1990

Bicycle manufacturer — Huffy Corp, Dayton, about thirty percent of the market

Campus — Ohio State University, Columbus

Patent suit settlement — the $125 million that a dispute over Duncan Hines crisp and chewy cookies crumbled into the coffers of Cincinnati's **Procter & Gamble,** 1989

Greeting card maker (publicly-owned) — American Greetings, Cleveland

Milk production by Jersey cow — 271,000 pounds, from Pansy, born December 9, 1965, William Diley farm, Canal Winchester

Roller Coaster selection — the Cedar Point nine, namely Blue Streak, Cedar Creek Mine, Corkscrew, Gemini, Junior Gemini, Iron Dragon, Wildcate, Magnum XL-200, Disaster Transport

Indoor ice surface — 200 x 172 feet, Winterhurst Municipal Ice Rink,
Lakewood

Water-powered grist mill —
Clifton Mill, Clifton

## Longest

Chicken flight — 302 feet, 6 inches, 1979 by Lola B., Bob Evans Farm Chicken Flying Meet, Rio Grande

Hand-operated navigation lock system — 93 miles of Muskingum River, Dresden-to-Marietta

Continuous TV show with one director — 1990 Otterbein College student broadcast, 48 hours, 13 minutes, 40 seconds

Indian effigy — 1254 foot long Great Serpent Mound, Ross County

Institutionalized — Martha Nelson, 99-year patient in Ohio state mental facilities

Ocean swim — Cuba-to-U.S., Walter Poenisch of Grove City, 1978

Overdue book — treatise on febrile diseases checked out of University of Cincinnati Medical Library in 1823, returned by borrower's great-grandson in 1968; $2,646 fine waived

Pogo stick jumping — 177,737 continuous hops, Gary Stewart, Reading, 1990

*Rocky Horror Picture Show* run — 14 years, Graceland Cinema, Columbus

Trapline — 320 feet, at the Grand American Trap-shooting Tournament, Vandalia

### Smallest

Power boat to cross the Atlantic — thirty feet, piloted by Ed Gillespie, Columbus

Street — thirty-feet-long McKinley Street, Bellefontaine

Viticultural area — one square mile, Isle St. George

### Oldest

Continuous Christmas bird count — Harrison County, since 1900

Community foundation — the Cleveland Foundation, started in 1914

Lighthouse operating on Great Lakes — Marblehead, since 1822

Professional theatre — Cleveland Playhouse, founded 1926

University west of the Alleghenies — Ohio University, Athens, chartered 1803

Watercraft in North America — canoe circa 1600 B.C. found in Ashland County peat bog

Choral music festival — Cincinnati's May Festival, founded 1873

# Weather, or not

## Mean and magnificent moments

### Rainfall

Most — Chardon, average 45.22 inches per annum

Least — Put-in-Bay, average 30.96 inches per annum

Heaviest short term — Sandusky, 9.54 inches in eight hours, July 12, 1966

Average annual in

Cincinnati — 40.14 inches
Cleveland — 35.4 inches
Columbus — 36.97 inches
Toledo — 31.78 inches

### Snowfall

Most — Chardon, average 106 inches per season

Greatest single — Steubenville, 36 inches in three days, November, 1950

Accumulation, 1975-85

Cleveland — 627 inches
Dayton — 334.6 inches
Columbus — 316.9 inches
Cincinnati — 269.9 inches

Average seasonal snowfall, 1955-85

Cincinnati — 24 inches
Cleveland — 53.6 inches
Columbus — 28.4 inches
Toledo — 38.3 inches

### Temperature

Highest — 113°F, Centreville (Gallia County), July 21, 1934

Lowest — −39°F, Milligan (Perry County), Feb. 10, 1899

Warmest place — Ironton, average mean of 56°F

Coldest place — Dorset, average mean of 46.6°F

Average mean in
Cincinnati — 53.3°F
Cleveland — 49.6°F
Columbus — 51.6°F
Toledo — 48.5°F

## Tornadoes

Average number per year — 14

Average forward speed in Ohio — 25 to 40 miles per hour

Most active month — June, when about 25 percent occur

Most common time period — between 4 and 10 p.m.

Most likely direction — 90 percent come out of the southwest

## Wind

average speed in
Cleveland, 11.6 miles per hour
Akron-Canton, 10.4 miles per hour
Dayton, 10.3 miles per hour
Cincinnati, 9.6 miles per hour
Columbus, 8.2 miles per hour

## Cloudless days per annum

Akron, 70
Cincinnati, 80
Cleveland, 70

# Honorable mentions

**Going far afield with the good names of Ohio**

**"Akron"**
Akron-built ship that was the second rigid zeppelin (ZR-2) built for the Navy; crashed near New Jersey in 1933

**Benjamin Harrison Literary Society**
night club in Pittsburgh, Pennsylvania

**Bowling Green**
Geoffrey Beene fragrance for men

**Cincinnati Arch**
shallow bed of basement rock three thousand feet below western Ohio and eastern Indiana (also called Ohio-Indiana platform)

**Cleveland Shale**
fossil-rich gray shale deposited near Cleveland by a sea 350,000,000 years ago that also left behind the skeletons of *Dunkleosteus* (a 20 foot fish) and *Cladoselache* (an early shark)

**General Sherman**
the giant sequoia in Sequoia National Park, California, that is the largest living thing on earth (274.9 feet tall; weight 2800 tons) and named for Lancaster's William Tecumseh Sherman

**McGuffey Lane**
Country-rock group taking its name from a street in Athens

**Mt. McKinley**
Alaskan mountain named for William McKinley that is the highest peak (20,320 feet) in the United States

### Mt. Beard
beside Mt. McKinley; named for Cincinnati-born Daniel Carter Beard, who helped start the Boy Scouts of America

### Portsmouth Shale
Gray shale deposits of Scioto County that once yielded the best paving bricks in the United States

### Shawnee
crater that is the only feature on the Martian landscape named after an Ohio town. Shawnee, Mars, is 9.9 miles across; Shawnee, Ohio measures 1 x 1.7 miles

### "Spirit of Columbus"
Cessna 180 airplane that Jerrie Mock of Columbus flew on her 1964 record-setting solo flight around the world

### "Spirit of Dayton"
balloon that Al Nels, Beavercreek, piloted to win the National Hot Air Balloon Championship in 1984 and 1985

### Urbana, Champaign County, Illinois
named after Urbana, Champaign County, Ohio

### U.S.S. Lansdowne
Navy ship that carried the Japanese surrender party to the *Missouri* at the end of World War II; named for Greenville's Zachary Lansdowne, Navy captain who died in the crash over Ohio of his ship, the *Shenandoah* (ZR-1), the Navy's first zeppelin

***U.S.S. Ohio; U.S.S. Columbus; U.S.S. Cincinnati;
U.S.S. Toledo; U.S.S. Cleveland; U.S.S. Dayton; U.S.S.
Lorain County; U.S.S. Pickaway***
United States Navy ships

***Youngstown Kitchens***
metal kitchen cabinets popular in the 1950's;
made by Mullins Manufacturing, Warren

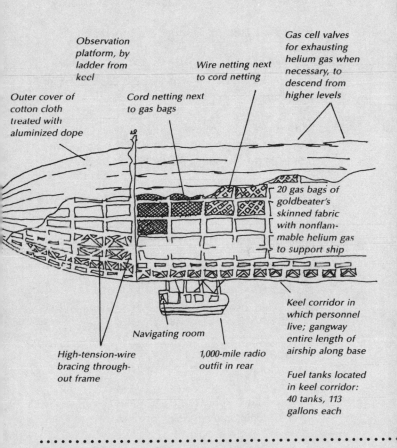

Observation platform, by ladder from keel

Wire netting next to cord netting

Gas cell valves for exhausting helium gas when necessary, to descend from higher levels

Outer cover of cotton cloth treated with aluminized dope

Cord netting next to gas bags

20 gas bags of goldbeater's skinned fabric with nonflammable helium gas to support ship

Navigating room

Keel corridor in which personnel live; gangway entire length of airship along base

High-tension-wire bracing throughout frame

1,000-mile radio outfit in rear

Fuel tanks located in keel corridor: 40 tanks, 113 gallons each

The Shenandoah was the first helium-filled, lighter-than-air rigid airship built in America. It cost $3 million to build — from plans of the German L-49 captured in World War I — and its 680-foot envelope was housed in a Lakehurst hangar that cost $3.5 million. Its lining of goldbeater's skin contained intestines from 750,000 oxen. Its diameter at midsection was 79 feet; it weighed 85 tons; and its maximum speed was 60 miles per hour. In its two years of existence, it was called the most successful airship in the world.

# One of a kind

Animal export station (privately owned) in U.S. — *Airborne Express,* Wilmington, depot for up to 350 cows, 40 horses, and 700 goats, sheep, or pigs

State that exports Hondas to the Japanese — *Ohio*

White lion in U.S. — the lioness *Joany,* Columbus Zoo

Diner owned by an historical society — *Joe's,* the Akron landmark whose deed is in the preserving hands of the Summit County Historical Society

Hippoquarium — *Toledo Zoo*

Independent piano plate foundry in North America — the *O.S. Kelly Company* of Springfield

Instrument landing system calibrators in U.S. — technician *John Luczak* and engineer *Taun Lam,* Newark Air Force Base

Metal whistle factory in U.S. — *American Whistle Corp,* Columbus

Mirrored lawn ornament ball maker — *Marietta Silver Globe Manufacturing,* Pinehurst

Municpally owned/operated hostel in U.S. — *Wintergarden Youth Hostel,* Bowling Green

Papal seminary in U.S. — **Pontifical College Josephinum,** Columbus

Pure white draft horse breeder — **David McCafferty,** West Farmington

Roller coaster turning riders upside down *six* times — **VORTEX,** Kings Island

Full-sized wooden carousel horse maker in U.S. — **Art Ritchie,** Mansfield

Big Ten quarterback to win the Heisman Trophy — **Les Horvath** of Ohio State, 1944

Football player who won the Heisman Trophy in consecutive years — **Archie Griffin,** Ohio State, 1974 and 1975.

Zip code with a single repeating digit — **Newton Falls,** 44444

# Down on the farm

*Ohio the bountiful, God bless her*

### Rome Beauty Apple

There was a maverick among the apple trees that Joel Gillett took down the Ohio River in 1816. When he got them home to Proctorville, all the grafts took, except for one tree that sprouted from the rootstock. Mr. Gillett knew it wouldn't produce the variety of fruit he wanted, so he gave the tree to his son, who planted the reject as far from the orchard as he could. The tree flourished, and to the Gilletts' surprise produced a remarkable apple — very round, bright red, and quite tasty. The apple became locally popular, and the Putman nursery in Marietta was so impressed that it bought the rights to grow the fruit. The nursery also gave the apple the name that **George Walton** suggested, Rome Beauty — Rome for the township where Gillett planted the first tree, and beauty for the obvious attributes of the once-scorned fruit. Gillett's original tree thrived, by the way, until it was destroyed by an Ohio River flood in 1860.

### Bees

When Amos Ives Root gave lectures on beekeeping, he used to tell his audiences that he had a sure cure for baldness. He slid open a draw, and enough bees flew out to cover his head. Now *that* was knowing his subject intimately, a skill that Mr. Root couldn't help himself from honing razor-sharp. Of his inquisitiveness, he once wrote, "I have ridden more hobbies and pushed them day and night, uphill and down, summer and winter . . ." Root's interest in bees became piqued in 1865 when a swarm flew past his jewelry store in Medina. He gave a man a dollar to catch the bees, and a year later, Root had pushed his fancy far enough to switch permanently from jewels to bees. He studied them assiduously, making observations and discoveries that allowed bees to be domesticated for commercial use. His work earned him the title *Honey King of America*, and his most popular innovation was a hive that allowed honey to be removed while leaving the comb intact. From Medina, A. I. Root Company sent bee-keeping supplies around the world. Root wrote a definitive book for apiarists, *The ABCs of Bee Culture*, and to keep them up-to-date, he started a magazine, *Gleanings in Bee Culture*, which he printed on a press powered by a windmill. In 1904, his subscribers were the first in the world to read of the Wright Brothers' flights in an article Root titled, "What Hath God Wrought?" The rhyme and reason of the Almighty, of course, remains as elusive as ever, but what Root wrought in Ohio is today fairly obvious — the majority of the nation's beekeepers, some 10,000 strong.

### Poland China Hog

In the early part of the nineteenth century, members of the Millennium Church of United Believers in the Second Coming of Chirst lived on choice farmland near Lebanon, Warren County. Commonly called *Shakers* for the bodily frenzy of their worship, they were a communal folk who denounced private property and practiced celibacy. In 1816, the Shakers imported from the East a meaty hog called the Big China, which they bred with Ohio's flinty razorbacks. Their experiments in crossing the fat with the lean over three decades resulted in a new and highly successful breed of hog. In 1876, the Swine Breeders Association called the new breed Poland China, a reference to both the roots of the animal and to those of *Asher Asher*, the Polish immigrant farmer who popularized the breed in Ohio as the non-reproducing Shakers died off. Within two years, the Poland China boar, King Tecumseh, was auctioned for $500, and in the early 1900's, The Pickett sold for the astounding — and record-setting — price of $60,000.

### Tomatoes

After nearly two decades of trial and error breeding, Alexander Livingston of Reynoldsburg in 1870 introduced the first *palatable* tomato — large, smooth-skinned, pleasantly tangy, and of fair color and size. He called his tomato the Paragon, an apt name, for before he introduced it, tomatoes were universally decried as tough and insufferably sour. Most folks thought them poisonous, and the tiny "Love Apples" were tolerated only as a garden ornamental. Livingston's tasty, fleshy Paragon launched the tomato industry, which became so important to Ohio agriculture that farmers dubbed large specimens **The Mortgage Lifter.** Having developed more than thirty varieties of tomatoes before his 1898 death, Livingston was the pacesetter for folks like Bonnie Tewart of Wayne who grew a tomato so spoilage-resistant that the Burpee Seed Company markets it as the Long-Keeper. At Ohio State's Agricultural Research and Development Center in Wooster, Dr. Stanley Berry developed two highly successful commercial tomatoes — Ohio 7814 and Ohio 7870 — that are firm, disease-resistant, and easily separated from the vine. Tomatoes, of course, are Ohio's backyard garden staple, and the state ranks second in the nation in the production of processing tomatoes, many of which are Ohio 7814 and Ohio 7870.

## Trophy vegetables

*1842* Issac Price, Mercer County, has a pumpkin seven feet in circumference which produces 170 pounds of *seeds*.

*1909* W. H. McKloskey, Perry Township, consents to have his thirteen-and-a-half pound radish put on display in the window of a local grocery.

*1910* Frank Fitzpatrick, Sidney, is astonished to find in his fruit cellar a potato sprout that is ten feet long.

*1934* On June 25, Andy Brunn declares that he is the winner of a three-man gardening race in Sidney. Brunn, age 86, says he sold his first potatoes Saturday and his first ripe tomato Monday, thereby defeating both Pete Scherer, who just has tomatoes, and Max Carey, who only has potatoes.

*1935* C. A. Poole of Shelby County picks a strawberry 2.25 inches wide and 2.40 inches long, which he brings to the attention of the local press along with the news that his strawberry yield is especially good.

*1977* With horse manure and a blue blanket to keep the plant warm at night, Mark and Randy Ohlin of Poland produce the world's longest gourd — eighty-two inches.

*1983* Thelva Thompson has to climb a twelve-foot ladder to harvest the Early Girl tomato plant growing up the side of her barn in Portsmouth;

*1986* Eric Mettle, Suffield Township, Portage County, delivers Ohio's biggest pumpkin: 434 pounds, eight ounces; Tom Mitchell, Akron, grows the biggest squash: 237 pounds, eight ounces;

# Inventory

## Our favorite Ohio inventions

**Airplane**
Wilbur and Orville Wright of Dayton, 1903

**Artificial Fish Bait**
Ernest Pflueger, Akron, 1883

**Automatic Traffic Signal**
Garrett A. Morgan, Cleveland, 1923

**Automobile Self-Starter**
Charles F. Kettering, Dayton, 1911

**Beer Can**
John Leon Bennett of Newark, 1937

**Bicycle**
"Velocipede" first patented by Fisher A. Spofford and Matthew G. Raffington, Columbus, October 5, 1869

**Book Matches**
Ohio Columbus Barber of Diamond Match Co., Barberton, 1896

**Cash Register**
James S. Ritty, Dayton, 1879

**Carbonless Copy Paper**
NCR Corporation, Dayton, 1955

**Circular Life Saving Net**
Thomas F. Browder, Greenfield, 1887

**Disposable Diapers (Pampers)**
Procter & Gamble, Cincinnati, 1962

**Disposable Vacuum Cleaner Bag**
Robert Lay Hallock of Columbus

**Do Little or Nothing Machine**
**(which has no apparent use)**
H. B. Shriver, Savannah, 1983

**Electric Dental Gold Annealer**
Dr. Luzern Custer, Dayton, 1890

**Electrolytic Process for Extracting Aluminum**
Charles Hall, Oberlin, 1886

**Ethyl Gasoline**
Thomas Midgely, Dayton, 1920's

**Floating Soap (Ivory)**
Procter & Gamble, Cincinnati, 1879

**Incandescent Electric Light Bulb**
Thomas Edison of Milan, 1879

**Manure Spreader**
Joseph Oppenheim, Mercer County

**Mechanical Corn Picker**
John W. Lambert, Ansonia, 1876

**Menthol Cigarette**
Lloyd "Spud" Hughes, Mingo Junction, 1920's

**Motorized Spaghetti Fork**
William Miscavich and Paul Shutt, Canton, 1969

**Play-Doh**
Tien Liu and Joseph McVicker, Cincinnati, 1950's

**Pop-Top Can**
Ermal Fraze, Dayton, 1965

**Preparation H**
Dr. George Sperti, Cincinnati, 1950's

**Pressurized Space Suit**
Russell Colley of Cuyahoga Falls, 1950's

**Reaper**
Obed Hussey, Cincinnati, 1833

**Regrigerator with Door Shelves**
"The Shelvador", Powel Crosley, Jr., Cincinnati

**Revolving Bookcase**
Joseph Danner, Akron

**Self-Lowering Toilet Seat**
Gregory Janek, Conover, 1986

**Stepladder**
John Balsley, Dayton, 1870

**Tapered Roller Bearing**
Henry Timken, Canton, 1898

**Vacuum Cleaner**
Murray Spangler, Canton, 1907

9137

♥ Ohio-born ***Thomas Edison*** patented more than a thousand inventions, including an electric vote recorder, the phonograph, the electric light, and "talkies." Congress cited him for having "revolutionized civilization"; he discovered the Edison Effect (electricity flow in a vacuum lamp); and folks called him a wizard. And yet, he was nominated for a Nobel Prize only once.

"Anything that won't sell, I don't want to invent."

***Thomas Edison***

offord & Raffington— *Velocipede*

# National standings

**First** in

    number of agricultural fairs

    number of 4-H clubs

    spelt (a feed grain) production

    canola production

    truck production

    number of Japanese auto part manufacturers

    total cash donations to reduce the public debt

**Second** in

    number of 4-H volunteers

    number of state park visitors

    automobile production

    processing tomato production

    number of historic properties

    potted cutting geranium sales

**Third** in

    number of tourists

    chrysanthemum production

    deaths occurring at railroad crossings

    industrial toxic chemical pollution

    exports to international markets

    child labor law violations

    potted Easter lily production

    potted poinsettia production

**Fourth** in

    number of household water wells

    egg production

    creamed cottage cheese production

    number of food stamp recipients

    number of metropolitan areas

    number of zoos

    union membership in manufacturing

**Fifth** in

number of divorces
number of slaughterhouses
sweet corn production
soybean production

**Sixth** in

number of marriages
number of shopping centers
number of farms
ice cream production
chicken population
number of lightning deaths

**Seventh** in

number of toll-road miles
number of prisoners executed, 1930-1988
number of millionaires
milk cow population
number of tornado deaths

**Eighth** in

Department of Defense spending in-state
oat production
Jewish population
number of registered boats

**Ninth** in

deaths from breast cancer
onion production
tobacco production

**Tenth** in

lowest average annual cost of auto insurance
apple production
domestic travel expenditures
strawberry production

# The essential books

## Several folks you should have over for dinner

**Lee Allen**

baseball's pre-eminent mid-century historian whose book, *The Cincinnati Reds*, is plainly titled, and anything but on the inside. It is a careful history of baseball's first professionals, and thus American baseball, as well as fun to read. Very few sources will tell you of the Reds' outfielder whose arm was so poor he once ran in with the ball and — in one prodigous flying leap — tagged the runner out at home plate.

**Sherwood Anderson**

of course, Ohio's foremost man of letters whose *Winesburg, Ohio* is the essential news about the state — and every other small town in America. It is bittersweet, with an unwavering gaze that disturbed, at the time, those caught in it. But, the book isn't as dirty as you heard, and not as straightforward, either.

**John Baskin**

believes Ohio is the center of the universe, a notion he espouses in *New Burlington: The Life and Death of an American Village* and *In Praise of Practical Fertilizer*. Harrison Salisbury said that "a better eulogy to real American people had never been written" than *New Burlington*, which evokes the enormous dignity of everyday folks in a southwest Ohio village. *In Praise of* is a collection of nearly seventy country essays in which Baskin — with wit and ruthless observation — builds a small universe from the most elementary topics. You won't know what it is to *sweat* until you've read his essay "Heat."

**Joan Chase**

whose *During the Reign of the Queen of Persia*, an elegaic novel of three generations of women on their northern Ohio farm, is as gifted as it is pleasurable. It is set in Ohio, yet straight in the tradition of the southern story-tellers, Flannery O'Connor and Eudora Welty.

### Dr. Gustav Eckstein

who taught medicine in Cincinnati and wrote in 1970 a symphony of essays called *The Body Has A Head*, which details in the most amazing and ardent ways the manner in which man is constructed. The intent, said Dr. Eckstein, "is to make the human body more familiar to anyone who owns one." He is a wonderful stylist, father to the more recent essayists Selzer and Thomas, and every bit as resourceful.

### Julia Foraker

the wife of Ohio governor and turn-of-the-century senator, Joseph "Fire Alarm" Foraker. Her memoirs, *I Would Live It Again*, is a splendid evocation of the late nineteenth century when Ohio commanded the country. It's a surprisingly well-written book, and while written is 1932, is decidedly modern in tone. The jacket copy promises, "Delightfully indiscreet social reminiscences."

### William Gold

whose book, *Fathers* is a fine evocation of what is was like to grow up in Cleveland in the 1940's. The father visits his son in California and brings with him Cleveland and at least several truckloads of fine, old-fashioned Jewish-American guilt.

### Alvin Harlow

whose history, *The Serene Cincinnatians*, is probably the best Ohio city biography (although George Condon's *Cleveland: the Best Kept Secret* is a close second, being the kind of book that academics disparage while it gives you what you really want from Cleveland). Harlow's book is nearly forty years old and out of print, but a delightful, readable chronicle that parts the lace curtains of one of America's most genteel cities.

### Harlan Hatcher
a master of the panorama, whose broad portraits of Ohio are nonetheless replete with detail. Hatcher combines the authenticity of a scholar with a storyteller's bent for human interest. Look up *The Western Reserve* and *The Buckeye Country: A Pageant of Ohio* in your library.

### Walter Havighurst
Ohio's most elegant and readable historian, whose observation is matched only by his style and sense of detail. Try his bicentennial history, *Ohio*, or his book on the Ohio River, *River to the West: Three Centuries of the Ohio*.

### Josephine Johnson
whom you should invite for either *Now in November*, the novel which won her a Pulitzer Prize a half-century ago, or *The Inland Island*, a depiction of twelve months on a small spur of native Ohio and one of the best nature books ever written.

### Conrad Richter
whose trilogy — *The Trees*, *The Fields*, and *The Town* — is the best writing about what it was actually like to come into the Ohio frontier. His people do heroic things in a matter-of-fact way, and his protagonist is a woman whose counterparts may still be observed in certain backroad Ohio towns.

### Scott Sanders and Jack Matthews

two of the best current essayists in America, whose collections, respectively (and respectfully), *The Paradise of Bombs* and *Booking in the Heartland*, are graceful, witty, and intelligent; in short, classic examples of a genre fallen of late into disrepair. Do not ask what they are about; ask your bookstore to find them — both are recent.

### Helen Hooven Santmyer

the tenacious octogenarian who dazzled the New York publishing world with her best-seller *. . . And Ladies of the Club.* If you were daunted by the sheer size of that, read instead *Ohio Town*, her best book, a good but slighty rose-colored portrait of small-town Ohio life told from a position of privilege and good fortune.

### Charles Allen Smart

whose book, *RFD*, may still be found in used bookstores around Ohio and is a worthy addition to your Ohioana. *RFD* is a carefully observed — and written — book, a year's sojourn on an Ohio farm and a picture of how Highland County appeared to a man accustomed to brighter lights.

### James Thurber

America's long-wearing humorist who always took Ohio with him. Almost everything he wrote is recommended, especially *My Life and Hard Times* and his affectionate retrospective of Ohio, *The Thurber Album.* He is the master of flat-footed fantasy, the fairy godmother in a union suit, and an everyday world that is quickly capable of becoming askew and magical.

# Great appellations

## Nearby places with far away names

**Florida and Texas** — only twenty-five miles apart in Henry County

**Chesapeake** — Lawrence County place without the Bay, just the Ohio River

**Belfast** — Highland County; seventy miles from London

**Cuba** — Clinton County; fifty miles from London

**London** — Madison County seat

**Lima** (say Lime-a) — named for the South American source of quinine, an old staple of Allen County medicine chests; about 100 crow-flying miles from its usual partner Peru (say Pee-roo) over in Indiana

**Mantua** — Portage County village that knew no Napoleonic conquest

***Moscow*** — on-the-Ohio, about 175 miles from Russia

***Russia*** (say Roo-sha) — where snow vistas meant *deja vu* for French settlers who were veterans of the Napoleonic Wars

In 1969, Mr. William Spellacy of Cleveland decided to take his three grandsons on a tour of the world's capitols, a journey they accomplished in the remarkable span of four days by visiting ***Geneva*** (Fairfield County), ***Rome*** (Adams County), ***Lisbon*** (Columbiana County), ***Paris*** (Stark County), ***London, Dublin*** (Franklin County), ***Amsterdam*** (Jefferson County), ***Athens*** (Athens County), ***Berlin*** (Holmes County), and ***Warsaw*** (Coshocton).

### Brokensword

is the site of Colonel William Crawford's legendary encounter with hostile Indians in the county that bears his name. Lest he perish by his own sword, Crawford stuck the foil into a creek bank and broke off the handle. But the act didn't foil the Indians, who vengefully and hideously burned him at the stake.

### Delightful

it is said that in his pre-political preaching days James Garfield suggested the obvious for this Trumbull County hamlet.

### Fizzleville

is so small that folks know each other's dogs by name. The place is officially called Hiett in Brown County, but the nickname stuck after commerce fizzled out years ago. Oh well, where industry failed, imagination triumphed — residents now enjoy a wry fame promoted by bumper stickers (I Followed and I Found Fizzleville), a newsletter *Fizzleville Times*, and the Fizzleville Fair.

### Fly

*seems* pejorative to this Ohio River town and may have been inspired by the insects attracted to a local barn, but the folks in Monroe County prefer to think that the name was chosen for other attributes — short, easy to pronounce, and definitely hard to forget.

### Knockemstiff

has always been known as a brawling, bare-knuckles place. A hoary tale tells that after the Civil War Preacher Robert Evland rode into the Ross County hamlet and found two women pulling each other's hair out over a cheating man. Once Evland got the gals settled down, he told them, "What you ought to do is go get your man and knock him stiff." Sometimes folk think that a new name would improve Knockemstiff's image, like a few years ago when two fellows rode their horses into a local bar and Shady Glen got a sudden surge in popularity. But Knockemstiff is just too hard to beat.

### Phoneton

is a Miami County crossroads started by the Bell Telephone Company in the 1890's and for many years the nexus of long distance lines.

### Pee Pee

Peter Patrick had just finished defacing a tree with his initials, when local Indians of a proprietary bent took offense. Mr. Patrick hightailed it to Kentucky, but his vainglorious act was commemorated by Pee Pee Township and Creek in Pike County.

### Columbiana

was nearly named Columbianamaria, but conservative heads prevailed, and the county formed on March 25, 1803, pays tribute only to Christopher Columbus and Quenn Anna.

### Dull

reflects on neither the landscape nor the citizenry of Van Wert County; it is — yawn — merely taken from James Monroe Dull, who owned the land.

### Eaton, Preble County

the Barbary Pirates of Africa are indirectly responsible for both of these names. When the United States decided to stop them from picking off its ships and citizens, Captain Edward Preble was one of the naval officers sent to give the pirates a quick trouncing and General William Eaton helped as consul in Tunis and Navy representative in North Africa.

### Morrow

named for Ohio's first Congressman and early Governor, Jeremiah Morrow, this Warren County town was punned into immortality by Lew Sully's old vaudeville tune, *I Want to Go to Morrow.* ❤

### Willshire

Shipwrecked off the coast of Morocco, Captain James Riley was picked up by Arabs who made him a slave. William Willshire, an Englishman, bought his freedom, a kindness Riley repaid when he came to Ohio in 1820 and started a town in Van Wert County. Although quite successful in Ohio, Riley never lost his love for the sea, and in 1840, he made his final voyage, dying three days out of of New York.

♥ Final verse from *I Want to Go to Morrow*:
> "Now, if you start to Morrow, it's a cinch you'll land
> Tomorrow in to Morrow, not today, you understand
> For the train today to Morrow, if the schedule is right,
> Will get you in to Morrow about tomorrow night.
> Said I: 'I guess you know it all, but kindly let me say,
> How can I go to Morrow if I leave the town today?'
> Said he: 'You cannot go to Morrow any more today,
> For the train that goes to Morrow is a mile upon its way.'"

### President's names
Ohio has forty places named Washington, thirty-seven called Jackson, and thirty-eight (a U.S. record) named Madison.

# Classical allusions/literary inclusions

### Arcanum

means "secret" in Latin, but folks in this Darke County village make no secret of the fact that theirs is the only Arcanum in the U.S.

### Ai

has the shortest name in Ohio; once there were so many saloons that folks thought that the Fulton County hamlet was due for the same fate as the city Joshua destroyed and would become a "heap of ruin."

### Sodom

at a Trumbull County crossroads during an 1840 Temperance meeting, the response was lukewarm enough for a Preacher Fisher to compare the place to the ill-fated city of yore. Residents took the name, but not the hint.

### Kipling

grew up around a mine in Guernsey County. Local folks got its name from the newspapers of the day, writer Rudyard Kipling winning out over Admiral Dewey, Prime Minister Gladstone, and President McKinley.

### River Styx

bears the name of Hell's mythological stream because of a menacing swamp that Medina County settlers called "the infernal region."

# A presidential album

## Native sons: Ohio presides over America

The first of them were born in frontier Ohio towns. They fought in the Civil War, plowed, and made speeches full of oratorical flourishes about large, simple nineteenth-century truths. The beards disappeared before the turn of the century. The last of Ohio's presidents came from towns, and were the creators of the modern presidency — decisive, managed, and important. Or they were *supposed* to be.

In the fifty-three years between the Reconstruction Era and the Roaring Twenties, ten men inhabited the White House — seven from Ohio. No other state has had such a period of hegemony. If the general impression is of whiskers and small deeds, we forget the sheer peacefulness of their terms. Only one took us to war. New states were born. Industries flourished. Inventions emerged. The Ohioans presided over long periods of surface calm while the country came into the new century. What follows is a miscellany of images as the Buckeyes went about the White House, in that half-century when Ohio ruled the country.

**WILLIAM HENRY HARRISON**
9th President, March 4 – April 4, 1841
born Feb. 9, 1773, in Virginia
not a native Ohio son, but one adopted after the early 1790's when he came to fight Indian wars and settled in North Bend

**ULYSSES SIMPSON GRANT**
18th President, March 4, 1869 – March 3, 1877
born Apr. 27, 1822, in Point Pleasant, Ohio

**RUTHERFORD BIRCHARD HAYES**
19th President, March 4, 1877 – March 3, 1881
born October 4, 1822, in Delaware, Ohio

**JAMES ABRAM GARFIELD**
20th President,
March 4 –
September 19, 1881
born November
19, 1831, in
Orange, Ohio

## BENJAMIN HARRISON
   23rd President, March 4, 1889 – March 3, 1893
   born August 20, 1833, in North Bend, Ohio

## WILLIAM MCKINLEY
   25th President, March 4, 1897 – September 14, 1901
   born January 29, 1843, in Niles, Ohio

## WILLIAM HOWARD TAFT
   27th President, March 4, 1909 – March 3, 1913
   born September 15, 1857, in Cincinnati, Ohio

## WARREN GAMALIEL HARDING
   29th President, March 4, 1921 – August 2, 1923
   born November 2, 1865, in
   Corsica, Ohio

### "First Lady"

Lucy Webb Hayes, not Martha Washington, was the *first* First Lady. She acquired the title courtesy of Mary Clemmer Ames, a reporter who called her "the first lady of the land" in an account of President Hayes's inauguration. The working press liked the sound of it better than "Presidentess" and stuck the name not only on Mrs. Hayes but also her White House successors.

### "Smoked-filled room"

This phrase came into the language when Harry Daugherty, Warren Harding's campaign manager, accurately predicted how the Republicans would choose their Presidential candidate in 1920:

"I don't expect Senator Harding to be nominated on the first, second, or third ballots, but I

think we can afford to take chances that, about eleven minutes after two, Friday morning of the convention, when ten or twenty weary men are sitting around a table, someone will say, 'Who will we nominate?' At that decisive time, the friends of Harding will suggest him, and we can afford to abide by the result."

### *"Let the chips fall where they may"*

This chestnut was first uttered by New York Senator Roscoe Conkling, who in 1880 said of President Grant: "He will hew to the line of right, let the chips fall where they may."

### *"Keep the ball rolling"*

One gimmick of **William Henry Harrison's** highly staged 1840 campaign was a paper ball six feet in diameter plastered with slogans. As Harrison Whig supporters pushed the ball from town to town, they yelled, "Keep the ball rolling!"

U.S. President with the biggest head: *James Garfield,* hat size 7¾

Last U.S. President to have a beard: *Benjamin Harrison*

Last Presidential moustache: *Taft's* magnificent handlebar

Big babies: *Garfield* and *Harding* both weighed 10 pounds at birth.

Big Chief: *Taft,* at 6'2" and 332 pounds, the largest U.S. President.

*Taft's* prodigous pajamas
    Neck, 19 inches
    Sleeve, 34½ inches
    Chest, 53 inches
    Waist, 54 inches
    Hips, 58 inches

*William Howard Taft's* bulk
    broke a sedan chair in Hong Kong
    inspired New York bakers to bake him a ninety-two-pound Christmas pie
    rendered him a swell power hitter but a woeful base runner
    got him stuck in at least *two* bathtubs, once on a ship to Cuba and again in the White House (the Navy, which knows a thing or two about staying afloat, came to his rescue with a forty-one-inch wide tub).

    "The biggest Babe I ever had — he looked like a red Irishman." *Garfield's* mother on his birth.

## Afflictions

*Hayes:* maniaphobia (fear of going insane) as a youth

*Garfield:* chronic depression in youth; indigestion; headaches and nightmares after elected President

*Benjamin Harrison:* physical exhaustion in 1867

*McKinley:* physical exhaustion during college

*Taft:* dengue fever in the Phillipines, 1901; heart strain from overweight; depression during Presidency

*Harding:* nervous breakdown, age 24, treated at Battle Creek sanitarium by Dr. J. Kellogg of the breakfast cereal family; frequent indigestion and heartburn

*Grant* relied upon his wife Julia to cure his fearsome headaches with mustard plasters and the dubious chemistry of her "little pills." Legend has it that when he arrived at Appomattox to meet Confederate General *Robert E. Lee,* the Union leader was suffering from a migraine that had begun two days before. As soon as he read Lee's letter of surrender, Grant's headache vanished.

The sight of blood made *Grant* so squeamish that he couldn't stand to look at the hides in his father's tannery. Meat cooked rare made him sick, and he refused to eat fowl. "I could never eat anything that went on two legs," he said. Ironically, Grant, who abhorred blood, led the Union Army in the nation's bloodiest internal conflict: the Civil War cost more than 600,000 lives.

Puttering

Teeing up.

The swish of the big-stick

Holed out in six.

FORE!!!

Well wasn't that a peach.

Of all the punk shot

President Taft's great girth prevented him from putting the ball on the tee. His presidential partner below is Harding, who had a different handicap.

It was **Harding's** custom to play golf at least twice a week. On July 2, 1921, he formally ended World War I in his golf clothes. An aide called the President off a New Jersey golf course, and he signed the resolution ending hostilities between Germany and the U.S. "That's all," said Harding before heading back to his game.

A friend of **Grant's** volunteered to introduce him to the game of golf. When they arrived at the course, a man was doggedly swinging at the ball, but couldn't quite manage to hit it.

"That does look like very good exercise," said the President to his friend. "But what is the little white ball for?"

**Alice Roosevelt Longworth** describes the **Harding** poker parties

"No rumor could have exceeded the reality; the study was filled with cronies . . . the air heavy with tobacco smoke, trays with bottles containing every imaginable brand of whiskey stood about, cards and poker chips ready at hand — a general atmosphere of waistcoat unbuttoned, feet on desk, and spittoons alongside.

**Grant** did not appreciate music. "I know only two tunes," he once said. "One of them is *Yankee Doodle,* and the other one isn't."

Nor did he dance, though he allowed that he "could dance if it were not for the music."

"We drew a pair of deuces and filled." — **Harding** on learning that the Republican Party had nominated him for President.

After being operated on for an ultimately fatal assassin's bullet, **McKinley** requested solid food and a cigar; doctors approved the former, denied the latter.

A crony describes President **Harrison** up a creek: "When he's on a fishing trip, Ben takes his drink of whiskey in the morning, just like anyone else. He chews tobacco from a plug he carries in his hip pocket, spits on his worm for luck, and cusses when the fish gets away."

**Garfield's** hobbies: hunting, fishing, billiards, and chess.

*Taft,* the former second baseman, started the tradition of the President opening the baseball season by tossing out the first ball. He did it on April 14, 1910, in an American League game between Washington and Philadelphia, and the crowd of 12,226 broke all attendance records.

*Harding* once wagered — and lost — a set of china that had been in the White House since the days of Benjamin Harrison. After the abuse of office scandals unfolded after Harding's death, his Poker Cabinet permanently cashed in its chips.

*Grant* was a heavy drinker. During the Civil War, he turned the tide of battle in the Union's favor, but was also rumored to enjoy sampling the liquor that his men slipped inside their rifle barrels. According to one apocryphal story, when *Lincoln* received reports that his winning general was falling off the wagon, he said, "If I knew what brand Grant used, I'd send every other general in the field a barrel of it."

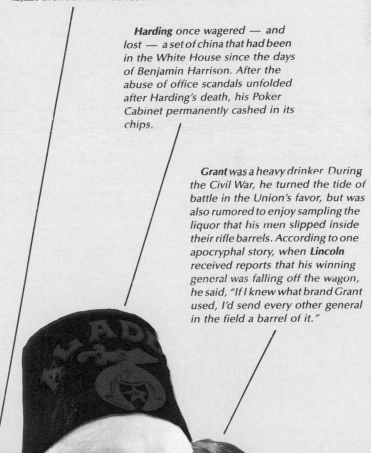

*W. H. Harrison*

---

**William Henry Harrison** was the first

(and only) Chief Executive who studied medicine

President-elect who traveled by train to Washington, D.C.

President photographed in office

to die in office, April 4, 1841

President who was the grandfather of a President, Benjamin Harrison.

**W. H. Harrison** on the Presidency

"Some folks are silly enough as to have formed a plan to make a President of the United States out of this Clerk and Clodhopper."

"All the measures of the Government are directed to the purpose of making the rich richer and the poor poorer."

♥

*Give him a barrel of hard cider and a pension, disdained one editor about Harrison, "and, our word for it, he will sit the remainder of his days in a log cabin by the side of a 'sea coal' fire and study moral philosophy." Thus was born the Great Cider Campaign of 1840.*

**Grant** was the first

President born in Ohio

to run against a woman, Victoria Claflin Woodhull from Ohio, nominated by the Equal Rights Party for the 1872 election

to receive a reigning king, David Kalakaua of Hawaii, on December 15, 1874.

**Grant** on the Presidency

"It was my fortune, or misfortune, to be called to the office of Chief Executive without any previous political training . . ."

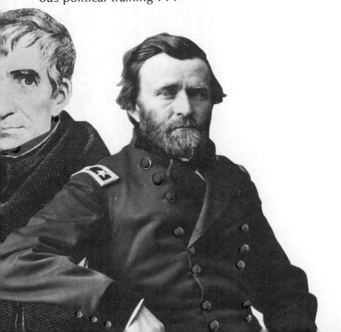

_R.B.Hayes_ (signature)

---

**Hayes** was the first

to take the oath of office in the White House; March 3, 1877, in the Red Room

who visited the West Coast while in office, arriving September 8, 1880, in San Francisco

to use the desk in the Oval Office, a gift from Queen Victoria in 1880.

**Hayes** on the Presidency

"He serves his party best who serves the country best."

"Nobody ever left the Presidency with less regret, less disappointment, fewer heartburnings, or more general content with the results of his term (in his own heart, I mean) than I do."

# DEMOCRATS
## 'PUT UP'
## —OR—
## SHUT UP
## I Want to BET From
## $100 to $500!
### THAT R. B. HAYES

Will be elected President of the United States of America. The money is now deposited at the office of the HERALD AND UNION.

Nov. 6th, 1876.   GEORGE MARLETTE

_J. A. Garfield._

---

**_Garfield_** was the first

to have his mother present at his inauguration

left-handed — and ambidexterous — President.

In 1880, while serving as an Ohio Congressman, **_Garfield_** was elected to U.S. Senator in January and then President in November. His senatorial and presidential terms were scheduled to begin on the same day — March 4, 1881, but Garfield, wishing to violate neither the laws of physics nor of propriety, resigned his House seat and chose the Presidency.

The beneficiary of a classical education, Garfield could write Greek with one hand at the same time that he wrote Latin with the other.

**_Garfield_** on the Presidency

"My God! What is there in this place that a man should ever want to get into it?"

"The President is the last person in the world to know what the people really want and think."

❤
Garfield appointed Cincinnati author, General Lew Wallace, to office, thinking of sending him to Paraguay. After reading Wallace's Ben-Hur, however, Garfield decided to send him to Constantinople, hoping he might find proper inspiration to write another biblical epic.

_Benjamin Harrison_ was the first

(and only) President who was the grandson of a President, William Henry Harrison

(and only) President to be preceded and followed in office by the same person, Grover Cleveland

Chief Executive with a billion dollar budget appropriated by Congress

to put up a Christmas tree in the White House, 1889

to have electricity in the White House, 1891.

President and Mrs. Harrison were so leery of electricity that they refused to touch switches. They left the lights on all night and had the servants turn them off in the morning.

_B. Harrison_ on the Presidency

"The President is a good deal like the old camp horse that Dickens described; he is strapped up so he can't fall down.

_"Cheer up, everybody. This is no life and death affair. I am very happy here in Indianapolis . . . "_

80

*WmMcKinley*

**McKinley** was the first

presidential candidate to campaign via the telephone; in 1896 he called campaign managers in 38 states from his Canton home.

**McKinley** on the Presidency

"I have had enough of it, heaven knows! I have had all the honor there is in this place, and have had responsibilities enough to kill any man."

*Taft* was the first

former cabinet member (Secretary of War under Theodore Roosevelt) to become President who was *not* a secretary of state

(and only) President to become Chief Justice of the U.S. Supreme Court, appointed June 30, 1921 by Harding.

*Taft* on the Presidency

"Politics makes me sick."

"Don't sit up nights thinking about making me President, for that will never come and I have no ambition in that direction. Any party which would nominate me would make a great mistake."

"I have come to the conclusion that the major part of the President is to increase the gate receipts of expositions and fairs and bring tourists into the town."

"The nearer I get to the inauguration of my successor, the greater the relief I feel."

♥

*In addition to several 'firsts,' Taft was also responsible for a notable White House 'last': Last milk cow in residence. Her name was Pauline Wayne, a most faithful servant.*

*W. G. Harding*

---

*Harding* was the first

   newspaper editor elected President

   U.S. Senator still in office when he got the White House

   President chosen in an election where women voted nationwide

   Chief Executive whose election was announced on radio (November 2, 1920, at KDKA, Pittsburgh)

   to ride to his inauguration in an automobile

   President who could drive an automobile

   President who owned a radio (purchased in 1922 and placed in his study)

   post Civil War President to advocate Black civil rights while south of the Mason Dixon line (at the University of Alabama, 1921)

   with a cabinet member convicted of a crime; in 1929, former Secretary of the Interior Albert B. Fall got one year in prison and a $100,000 fine for accepting bribes.


*Harding* on the Presidency

   "When I was a boy I was told that anybody could become President; I'm beginning to believe it."

   "I am a man of limited talents from a small town. I don't seem to grasp that I am President."

Father of His Country: **William Henry Harrison,** the U.S. President with the most children born of one marriage — 10 (six boys, four girls)

Grandfather of His Country: **William Henry Harrison,** a record 48 grandchildren and 106 great-grandchildren

Only man who was both the son and father of a U.S. President: **John Scott Harrison** of North Bend, Ohio; son of William Henry Harrison, father of Benjamin Harrison

First mother to attend her son's Presidential inauguration and to live in the White House: **Eliza Ballou Garfield**

**Garfield's** first act as President: kissing his mother

**Anna Symmes Harrison**
    was the only woman who was the wife of one U.S. President and the grandmother of another, William Henry Harrison and Benjamin Harrison
    was the oldest woman to become First Lady — 65 years, 222 days
    is the only wife of an Ohio President who never lived in the White House; he died before she could arrive from North Bend
    became the first Presidential widow awarded a pension, $25,000 from Congress in 1841

### Lucy Webb Hayes

was the first First Lady with a college diploma, graduated with honors from Ohio Wesleyan Women's College, 1850

banned liquor from the Executive Mansion

started the White House Easter Egg roll

### Caroline Scott Harrison

began the White House custom of using orchids at state receptions

undertook the first White House renovation; armed with $35,000 from Congress, she attacked insects and rodents while fortifying the plumbing with sorely needed bathrooms

### Helen "Nellie" Taft

brought the cherry trees in Washington, D.C., on March 27, 1912, personally planting the first of 3000 cherry trees that she had persuaded the Japanese government to send to the United States

is the only U.S. President's wife buried in Arlington National Cemetery, in 1943

♥

*Taft, at this point having foresworn horseback-riding for a Stanley Steamer, rides in it with his family. At right, his four-man, special-order bathtub. At center, Garfield reads to his daughter, Molly.*

***Florence Kling DeWolfe Harding***

was the first wife of a President who worked with her husband, as circulation manager of the Marion (Ohio) *Star*

edited her husband's inaugural address

was the first First Lady to accompany the outgoing President to the Capitol on Inauguration Day

Married without their fathers' blessings: ***Anna Symmes Harrison, Julia Grant,*** and ***Florence Harding***

Because wealthy ***John Cleves Symmes*** disapproved of his daughter's marrying a soldier, Anna married ***William Henry Harrison*** on the sly while her father was attending to business in Cincinnati. When the outraged Mr. Symmes demanded to know how Harrison planned to support his daughter, the future President replied, "By my sword, sir, and my good right arm."

*When Yale offered Taft its Chair of Law, he respectfully declined, saying that his considerable girth really required a "Sofa of Law."*

⑥

The tenants: (1) Garfield, (2) William Henry Harrison, (3-4) McKinley, (5) Grant's boyhood home, and (6) Taft's Mt. Auburn home in Cincinnati.

87

### Stellar Performers

### General
Grant, Civil War

### Major General
William Henry Harrison, Northwest Territory Indian wars and War of 1812; Garfield, Civil War

### Brevet Major General
Hayes, Civil War

### Brevet Brigadier General
Benjamin Harrison, Civil War

### Low rank
McKinley, promoted from private to brevet major, Civil War

### No rank
Taft and Harding, who never served in the U.S. military

### First Blood
Grant was the first Union general to win a major Civil War victory (capture of Fort Donelson, February, 1862), person to command an army via telegraph, four-star general in the U.S. Army.

### Top Kick
In the Civil War, Hayes, a colonel, was commanding officer of McKinley, a brevet major.

"Fighting battles is like courting girls: those who make the most pretensions and are boldest usually win." — *Hayes*

"I am not a Julius Caesar, nor a Napoleon, but a plain Hoosier colonel, with no more relish for a fight than for a good breakfast and hardly so much." — *Benjamin Harrison*

"A good soldier must always do his duty." — *McKinley*

"Young as he was, we soon found out that in the business of a soldier, requiring much executive ability, young McKinley showed unusual and unsurpassed capacity, especially for a boy of his age. When battles were fought or service was to be performed in warlike things, he always filled his place." — *Hayes* rating *McKinley's* service in the Civil War

"A man might fire at you all day without your finding it out." — *Grant* on the short-range muskets used in the war with Mexico

*"Ah, you may be sure that there will be no jingo nonsense under my administration."*

*Faithful Party-Goers*

Democrat Ohio Presidents — 0

Whig Ohio Presidents — 1
   *William Henry Harrison*

Republican Ohio Presidents — 7
   *Grant, Hayes, Garfield, Benjamin Harrison, McKinley, Taft, Harding*

Presidents elected without a popular-vote majority
   *John Quincy Adams,* 1824
   Ohioan *Rutherford B. Hayes,* 1876
   Ohioan *Benjamin Harrison,* 1888.

Republican *Hayes* garnered 4,036,298 votes in 1876. Democrat *Samuel Tilden* had more — 4,300,590 — but the 19 electoral votes of three southern states were in question. Congress appointed an electoral commission to settle the matter, and the members awarded Hayes the disputed votes, giving him the Presidency by a slim 185 to 184 margin.

In 1888, Democrat *Grover Cleveland* won a majority in the popular vote (5,444,337) to Harrison's 5,439,853, but not in the electoral college. *Harrison* carried 20 states with 233 electoral votes, while Cleveland's eighteen states tallied only 168.

The 1892 contest between *Benjamin Harrison* and *Grover Cleveland* was so lackluster that one observer remarked, "Each side would have been glad to defeat the other if it could do so without electing its own candidate."

## Lengthy deliveries

Average number of words used by Ohio Presidents in inaugural addresses: 3569.

Average number of words used by all U.S. Presidents in inaugural addresses: 2399.

U.S. record for longest inaugural address:
  *W. H. Harrison*
  Runner-up: *Taft*

Record for use of pronoun "I" in inaugural address: *W. H. Harrison*, 45 times.

"(McKinley) used too many hackneyed phrases, too many stereotyped forms. He shook hands with exactly the amount of cordiality and with precisely the lack of intimacy that deceived men into thinking well of him, too well of him."
— William Allen White

"His speeches left the impression of an army of pompous phrases moving over the landscape in search of an idea. Sometimes these meandering words would actually capture a straggling thought and bear it in triumphantly, a prisoner in their midst until it dies of servitude and overwork."
— William McAdoo on Harding.

*"I don't know what to do or where to turn in this taxation matter. Somewhere there must be a book that tells all about it, where I could go to straighten it out in my mind. But I don't know where the book is, and maybe I couldn't read it if I found it."*

*The hometown inauguration
of Mr. McKinley*

### William Henry Harrison

insisted on delivering his inaugural address in a snowstorm without a hat or coat. The elderly Harrison took an hour and forty-five minutes to deliver his record setting speech, promptly caught cold, and died of pneumonia a month later.

Thus, Harrison established that most suspect of political laws: the inverse ratio between long-windedness and term of office, for the President with the most to say also had the shortest term of office.

### Grant

took his second oath of office on a bitter March 4, 1873. The inaugural parade bogged down under blizzard-like snow, and West Point cadets fainted from the cold. Guests at the inaugural ball danced with their coats on, and the champagne froze.

### Garfield

braved deep snow and high winds for his inauguration, but Washington boulevards were cleared in time for the inaugural parade.

### Benjamin Harrison

took a page out of grandfather William Henry's book and rode an open carriage to the Capitol in a hard rain with stong winds. He survived, of course, although the fireworks scheduled for that evening did not.

### McKinley

had a fine parade for his first inauguration. A good thing, because his second in 1901 was dampened by a deluge. Also rained-out: the evening's fireworks.

### Taft

was chased inside the Senate Chamber to take his oath of office by a blizzard. Felled tree limbs blocked politicos from coming to Washington, and most of the parade marchers went home early.

*Theodore Roosevelt,* his predecessor, bolted tradition and instead of riding back to the White House with Taft, got on a train and left town, presumably while he still could, whereupon Mrs. Taft took his place beside her husband, starting a tradition of her own which First Ladies have been honoring ever since.

## Alma maters

**William Henry Harrison** — University of Pennsylvania (no degree)

**Grant** — U.S. Military Academy at West Point

**Hayes** — Kenyon College, Ohio

**Garfield** — Williams College

**Benjamin Harrison** — Miami University, Ohio

**McKinley** — Allegheny College (no degree)

**Taft** — Yale

**Harding** — Ohio Central College

Post graduates
  **Hayes** — Harvard, Law
  **Taft** — University of Cincinnati, Law

**Grant** was appalled when he learned that his father had arranged to have him appointed to West Point without his knowledge. The possibility of flunking out terrified him, and when his father insisted that he go, young Grant prayed that his steamboat would sink or his train wreck. At the Point, Grant set a record for the high jump on horseback and was elected president of the Dialectic Society, but his struggles with French, engineering, and military science put him 21st out of 39 in the Class of 1843. He also acquired a string of demerits for missing church, an unkempt uniform, and being late.

"A military life," he later said, "had no charms for me, and I had not the faintest idea of staying in the Army even if I should be graduated, which I did not expect."

# Landmark foods

## First in the stomachs of our countrymen

### The Hamburger

Canton grocer and itinerant cook **Frank Menches** claimed to have invented the hamburger in the 1890's at the Summit County Fair. Having run out of sausage for sandwiches, he told an assistant to "grind some beef," thus executing a truly grandstand play with a pinch hitter.

### The Hot Dog

Harry M. Stevens of Niles is credited with being the first person to wed weiner to bread; the union was blessed as a "hot dog" after a New York newspaper caricatured the frankfurter as a Dachsund in 1900.

### Johnny Marzetti

Into the world's waiting lips, Columbus also thrust this cafeteria classic, courtesy of the Marzetti restaurant. **Mary Marzetti** created her beef/cheese/tomato/macaroni casserole around the turn of the century and named it for her husband, Johnny.

### Chewing Gum

The Indians taught us to smoke *and* chew, but it took a Mount Vernon man to sew up the legal rights to their age-old habit of ruminating on spruce gum. On December 28, 1869, **William F. Semple** got the first patent for chewing gum, a flavored and sweetened chicle.

### Life Savers

Cleveland chocolate maker **Clarence Crane** invented Life Savers in 1912. He flavored the candies peppermint and sold them, at five cents, "for that Stormy Breath."

### Breakfast Cereal

When the Civil War started, **Ferdinand Schumacher** answered his country's call — not with arms, but with oatmeal. Until then about the only takers for oatmeal that he ground in his grocery store were Akron neighbors, but stomachs on the march demanded a nutritious food that traveled well. Schumacher's oatmeal was the perfect K ration. His cheap, quick-cooking cereal captured the Union's tastebuds so successfully that he became the "Oatmeal King of America" and his mills evolved into the giant Quaker Oats company. Quaker puffed rice and oats were advertised as being "shot from cannons," which, in retrospect, they truly had been.

### Rippled Potato Chips

Emerson Cain of Bowling Green claims he invented the first corrugated potato chips in the 1930's and coined the term "marcelle chips" because they resembled the popular wavy hairdo.

### American Champagne

Cincinnatian **Nicholas Longworth** experimented with thousands of grapes before he was introduced to the Catawba in 1825, a native "wonder" variety that not only tolerated cold weather but also produced a non "foxy" wine. American winemakers had searched for such a grape for decades, and from the Catawba, Longworth produced the nation's first champagne. By 1859, his vines stretched for miles around Cincinnati, and Ohio was the premier wine state, out-producing California two to one. Longworth heartily concurred with the observation that bringing the Catawba grape to public notice was a greater service to the country than paying off the national debt.

### Girl Scout Cookies

In 1930, Girl Scouts in Akron were one of the first in U.S. to engage a commercial bakery for their cookies. Albrecht Grocery Co. made nearly a hundred thousand sandwich cremes stamped with a picture of Peter Rabbit. The good scouts bagged and sold the cookies for a $480 profit, and within four years, all of the nation's Girl Scout cookies were bakery-made.

### Cincinnati Chili

Spaghetti and chili sauce topped variously with cheese, onions, and beans — thus, we have what is known in the local vernacular as a three-way, four-way, or five way. Macedonian Immigrant *Athanas Kiradjieff* takes the bows for inventing this Cincinnati passion at his first Empress restaurant in the 1920's.

### Ohio Lemon Pie

Shakers believed in Christ, simplicity, hard work, cleanliness, and celibacy. Aside from inventing clothes pins, the apple parer, the swivel chair, and the circular saw, they were probably the world's foremost promoters of the lemon, which they prescribed for chilbains, fevers, neuralgia, warts, dandruff, and gum disease.

### Black Pearl Wine

Available no where but the Steuk Wine Company, Sandusky, this is an Ohio original — made from the Black Pearl grape developed by Caspar Schraidt on South Bass Island and introduced at the Ohio State Fair in 1874.

# Quoteables

"The only good Indian is a dead Indian."
   Perry County's **Gen. Philip H. Sheridan,** to a Comanche Chief, 1869

"But hear me: a single twig breaks, but the bundle of twigs is strong. Someday, I will embrace our brother tribes and draw them into a bundle and together we will win our country back from the whites."
   **Tecumseh,** Shawnee Chief, August 12, 1810

"We've got them."
   **Gen. George Custer** of New Rumley, on the Sioux attack at the Little Big Horn, 1876

"We have met the enemy and they are ours — two ships, two brigs, one schooner, and one sloop."
   **Oliver Hazard Perry** to William Henry Harrison upon his victory at the Battle of Lake Erie, 1813

"Now he belongs to the Ages."
   **Edwin M. Stanton,** Cadiz lawyer and U.S. Secretary of War, on the death of Lincoln

"All the news that's fit to print."
   Cincinnati's **Adolph S. Ochs,** publisher of *New York Times*

"I'm just a lucky slob from Ohio."
   **Clark Gable** from Cadiz

"If you can't stand the heat, turn off the stove."
   Dayton City Commissioner **Abner Orick**

"Millions for manure, but not one cent for literature."
   **Joseph Villiers Denney,** dean of the Ohio State University College of Arts and Science

"The airplane stays up because it doesn't have the time to fall."

**Wilbur and Orville Wright,** Dayton

"That's one small step for a man; one giant leap for mankind."

**Neil Armstrong,** Wapakoneta, setting foot on the moon, July 20, 1969

"Genius is one per cent inspiration and ninety-nine per cent perspiration."

Milan-born **Thomas Edison**

"If Thomas A. Edison, the Wright Brothers, and Henry Ford had taken I.Q. tests, they wouldn't have gotten in the bleachers, let alone the grand-stand."

Dayton auto inventor and entrepreneur **Charles F. Kettering**

"I will not accept if nominated and will not serve if elected."

**William Tecumseh Sherman,** Civil War General from Lancaster, heading off the Republican presidential nomination, 1884

"Hold the fort. I am coming."

**William Tecumseh Sherman** to Gen. John Corse, under seige in Georgia, 1864

"War is hell."

**William Tecumseh Sherman,** who in an 1880 speech in Columbus actually said, "There is many a boy here today who looks on war as all glory, but boys, it is all hell."

# Cheap shots

## Some insubstantial, below-the-belt remarks

### At Cincinnati

"I'm sure I would have liked Cincinnati much better had the people not dealt largely in hogs . . . if I determined to walk up Main Street, the chances are 500 to one my reaching the shady side without brushing by a snout fresh dripping from the kennel . . ."

Frances Trollope, 1830's

"Elizabeth, if you don't love me no more, I'm moving to Cincinnati."

Robert Duvall's *Angelo, My Love*

"You are a young man from Cincinnati. What do *you* know?"

Danny Kaye film, *Skokie*

### At Cleveland

"What's the difference between Cleveland and the Titanic?

The Titanic had better restaurants."

old joke

"Cleveland is Detroit without the glitter."

old joke

"Cleveland suffers from an inferiority complex, and it's easy to see why. Outsiders have been laughing at her ever since some religious nut was seen walking the streets wearing a sandwich board that said, 'Lake Erie Died for Your Sins.'"

David Casstevens, Dallas reporter

"Can't we just move to Cleveland?"

*Amazing Stories* youth upon hearing that his family must move 92 billion miles into outer space

"Mother, Sammy Jo is everything you say she is. But it's a big world, and I haven't even hit Cleveland yet."

*Dynasty* television series, 1986

### At Dayton

"The Wright Brothers probably invented the airplane to have a quick way out of town."

Tim Sullivan, the *Cincinnati Enquirer*

"It seems to be a widespread and peculiar feeling, and I can't possibly understand it, that no writer could possibly live in Dayton, Ohio. I guess they think you're supposed to live in St. Moritz or someplace like that."

John Jakes, writer

"Back to that $35 a week job on the copy desk at the *Dayton Post* . . ."

William Holden, *Sunset Boulevard*

### At Large

"'Did you have to view him?'
'No. His relatives are coming from Ohio.'
'Suicide is very Ohio, you know.'
'I guess.' Hers, as always is a perfect Michigan attitude. No one there has any patience for Ohio."

*The Sportswriter*, Robert Ford

"Damnable Ohio sod! Must plough and till again."

*The Tree of Life*, Hugh Nissenson

"There goes one of those Georgia peaches. There's nothing like that back in Ohio."

carpetbagger observing Scarlett O'Hara,
*Gone With the Wind*

"Few youngsters running away to sea head to Toledo."

anonymous observer

"Munich is Akron with a crewcut."

columnist Jim Murray

"Yellow Springs sort of reminds me of a theme park, only I can't figure out what the theme is."

New York City visitor, 1985

"Ripley was badly infected with infidelity, Universalism, and whiskey retailers."

Abolitionist John Rankin

"A fussy old hen of a town forever clucking over its little brood of railroads . . ."

James Whitcomb Riley on Union City

"You go to the park and see the cannon, and you've had it. You go to the five and ten, look through that for a while. That's the end of the day. They've got one Chinese restaurant in town; it serves bread and butter, cottage cheese, and Fig Newtons for dessert."

Lenny Bruce on Lima

# Coronets

### Thanks for a warm hand
### on a cold morning

### On Cincinnati
"A beautiful city, cheerful, thriving, animated . . ."
   Charles Dickens, 1843

### On Cleveland
"Good town. Good people. Good time."
   Prince Napoleon, 1861

"Euclid Avenue is one of the finest streets in the world. The only thoroughfare to be compared to it is the Prospekt Nevsky in St. Petersburg."
   Bayard Taylor, 1860's

"The best governed city in the United States . . ."
   Lincoln Steffens, 1904

### On Dayton
"Dayton is a place where inventors and innovators are treated like baseball players."
   New York image consultant, 1985

"The only reason that I'm sane and syndicated by a lot of papers is that I live in Dayton, Ohio. I live in a spot where life goes on. No matter what happens in New York or Washington, Dayton, Ohio is still there."
   Pulitzer Prize winning cartoonist
   Mike Peters, 1986

## On the Whole

"Our position in the nation is peculiarly felicitous as we have soil, climate, and productions, and it will be our own fault if we are not the happiest people in the Union."

Caleb Atwater, 1838

"This is a good country, the Ohio country, and I have never ceased to be content that here I came to rest."

*The Autobiography of Judge Stacy Taylor*

"Now I am back in God's Country."

103-year-old Findlay expatriate upon her 1983 return

"Up until a year ago, the center of the Universe was a wood lot in Chester Township, which happened to be owned by an irascible old fellow name of Williams. I'm not exactly sure where it is now . . ."

John Baskin, Ohio author and chronicler

# Itchy feet

### Giving in to Wanderlust

**Neil Armstrong**
achieved ultimate traveler status when he became the first person to set foot on the moon. As command pilot of the *Apollo XI* mission, the Wapakoneta native emerged from the Lunar Module *Eagle* on to the Sea of Tranquility, July 21, 1969.

**Jedediah Strong Smith**
of Perrysville traveled with the Ashley-Henry Expedition of 1822, a fur-trading venture that opened new overland routes to the West. Smith, a "mountain man" trapper, became the first white man to reach California by land when he discovered the South Pass route. He was also the first to cross the Sierra Nevada and to explore the California-Oregon coastline by land.

**Ezra Meeker**
traveled the Oregon Trail to the Pacific three times. In 1851-52, the Huntsville man went by ox-pulled covered wagon; in 1914, by automobile; in 1923, by airplane.

**Laura Corrigan**
covered a lot of ground by being *upwardly* mobile. She was a milkmaid who became probably the most renowned international socialite of the 1920's. Her full name — Laura Mae Whitlock McMartin Corrigan — tells a lot about how she did it. When Laura married Jimmy Corrigan, the scion of a wealthy Cleveland family, he provided her with a lavendar Rolls Royce and liveried footman, a dramatic — but fitting — entrance for the woman known as the "Flagpole Kelly of Social Climbers."

### Grandma Gatewood

was a champion walker from Gallipolis. In 1959 at age 72, Emma Gatewood trekked 2200 miles to Lincoln City, Oregon.

### Charles F. Kettering

was a nuts-and-bolts genius whose automotive research and development — electric ignition, generator, and lights; variable speed transmissions; two-way shock absorbers — made travel cheaper and easier for millions of people. Yet, he was without a doubt Ohio's worst traveler, not because of *where* he went, but *how* he got there, which for a man preoccupied with invention was frequently late or not at all. On one occasion, Mr. Kettering boarded a train and couldn't find his ticket. "No problem," the conductor told his esteemed passenger, "just send us a check when you get home." "Hang the check," said Mr. Kettering. "I've got to find that ticket, or I won't know where I'm supposed to be going."

### Adib Karam and James Matz

worked their way around the world together in 1925. Leaving Akron with the munificent sum of one dollar, they traveled by wit and grit to the Sahara, Bombay, Peking, and the Pyramids, returning home with five cents, a loaf of bread, and the makings of a book, *A Vagabond Journey Around the World — On Nothing.*

### Walt Beckjord

is an inveterate walker familiar with backroads from Hamilton County to the Himalayas. In 1982, he ran for the U.S. Senate by walking; his knickers-and-walking stick campaign covered the length and breadth of Ohio, from Fountain Square in his hometown Cincinnati to Public Square in

Cleveland, where he stumbled over a fellow named Metzenbaum.

### Dwight Mitchell and Steve Kirk
set a world record in 1983, when the Dayton motorcyclists traveled 2945 miles in 74 hours and 37 minutes.

### Sharon Chrostowski
from Kent State University walked from San Francisco to Washington, D.C., during a 4000 mile trek sponsored by the American Hiking Society, 1979-1980.

### James J. Brady
of Wilmington bought an "All Aboard America" ticket in 1984 and used it to ride 25,980 miles of Amtrak rails in one month.

### Curtis White
rode an eighteen-speed bicycle from Lincoln City, Oregon, to Rehoboth Beach, Delaware, in 1986. The Miamisburg man traveled 3264 miles in 39 days.

### Parke Thompson
is an Akron attorney whom the **Guiness Book of World Records** calls "the most traveled living American." So far, he has visited 304 of the 308 places listed by the Travelers' Century Club. Mr. Thompson, who made his first trip to Europe at age six and traveled the 48 contiguous states as soon as he could afford a car, says that he collects countries the way other people collect stamps. Predictably, he also collects travel slides — some 80,000 and counting.

### Bart

hot dogged around Cincinnati, literally. Operating out of Arnold's Bar and Grill (he loved jazz and regarded Number 2 as his personal booth), the long and low mutt was a true man about town who attended to the needs of his varied and geographically diverse lady friends by riding downtown buses. Though Bart once got as far north as Finneytown, he died (happily, while on his way to a Main Street liaison) trying to cross Liberty Street.

### Steve Newman

was the first person to walk around the world alone. Leaving from his Bethel home on April 1, 1983, he returned four years and 22,500 miles later. Since then, he has received 2000 letters, retained an agent to handle endorsements and appearances, and had named in his honor the Steve Newman Worldwalker Perimeter Trail at East Fork State Park. Says Newman the Conqueror: "Can you believe that a hobo who spent all his time eating beans and sleeping under bridges is being treated like a king chauffered around in limousines and jets?"

# The annotated Ohio

## The lay of the land

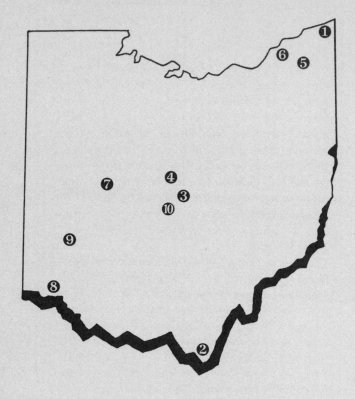

♥ "But where exactly
is Ohio? I have always
replied, 'It is the
farthest west of the
east, and the farthest
east of the west, the
farthest north of the
south, and the far-
thest south of the
north, and it is proba-
bly the richest area of
its size in the world.'"
— Louis Bromfield

Ohio owns 2,097,000 acres of **Lake Erie**

**1** Northernmost place — near **Conneaut,** approximate latitude, 41°58'

**2** Southernmost place — **South Point,** approximate latitude, 38°24'

Length (extreme north to south) — 205 miles

Width (extreme east to west) — 230 miles

**3** Geographic center — **Centerburg,** Knox County

**4** Demographic center — **Franklin Township,** Morrow County

320 miles of shoreline

35,000,000 walleye

10,907,000 people

41,222 square miles of territory

**5** Largest county — **Ashtabula,** 711 square miles

**6** Smallest county — **Lake,** 232 square miles

Counties with crookedest borders — **Washington** and **Noble,** approximately thirty corners each

**7** Highest point — **Campbell Hill,** Logan County, 1550 feet above sea level

**8** Lowest point — **Ohio River,** year Cincinnati, 433 feet above sea level

**9** Smallest incorporated town — **Jacksonburg,** population 50

**10** Largest city — **Columbus,** population 569,570

Counties with most bordering counties — **Stark,** 8 also Ashland, Ross, Licking, and Madison, 7

state historic places take up 5022 acres

lakes, ponds, and reservoirs account for 206,700 acres

44,000 miles worth of rivers and streams

farms occupy 14,997,000 acres

forests cover 7,100,000 acres

foreigners own about 170,000 farm acres

60 percent of everybody else is only a day's drive away

# Going native

## The tribal rites, signs, and ceremonies

State bird — the cardinal (***Cardinalis cardinalis***), adopted 1933

State flower — the **red carnation,** William McKinley's lapel favorite, adopted 1904, as a posthumous tribute

State motto — ***"With God All Things Are Possible,"*** from Matthew 19:26; adopted 1959 ❤

State nickname — ***The Buckeye State***

State slogan — ***"Ohio, the Heart of It All,"*** from a Columbus advertising agency, adopted 1984

State song — ***Beautiful Ohio,*** adopted 1969 ❤

State tree — the buckeye (***Aesculus glabra***), adopted 1953 ❤

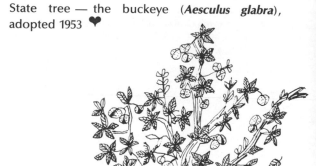

♥ Mottos are a matter not to be taken lightly, or quickly, in the case of Ohio. After deciding on the Great Seal, it took the state another sixty-two years to come up with a motto, *Imperium in Imperio*, meaning an "Empire within an Empire." But that struck a lot of folks as entirely too pretentious, and the "too royal" motto was recalled after only a couple of years. Ohio was mottoless until 1959 when this deficiency was brought to the attention of the state's schoolchildren. When twelve year-old *James Mastronardo* of Cincinnati suggested a Biblical line, he accomplished what several generations of solons couldn't. Ohio, at last, had a motto.

♥ *Beautiful Ohio* is an old vaudeville tune of alien parentage. Robert King, a New Yorker who used the pen name Mary Earl wrote the melody, while Oregon native Ballard MacDonald added the words several years later. This questionable background plus the fact that the song ("Long long ago/someone I know/Had a little red canoe/In it room for only two . . .") celebrated the river rather than the landscape prompted the General Assembly to have a state song contest in 1967. When the mail-in campaign showed just how comfortable an old shoe can be, legislators bowed to the peoples' overwhelming choice and made *Beautiful Ohio* official.

♥ The Latin words in the Buckeye tree's scientific name mean oak and smooth, but the Indians called the species "hetuck", meaning buckeye because the seeds so strongly resembled the eye of a male deer. When *Colonel Ebenezer Sproat* arrived at Marietta in 1788 to be the new sheriff, the Indians were highly impressed and honored him with the name Hetuck, thus making Sproat the first recorded Buckeye.

But not until a half century later did Ohioans in general acquire a national reputation as Buckeyes. During *William Henry Harrison's* 1840 presidential campaign, his opponent said that Harrison's Ohio roots suited him better for a log cabin than the White House. Now, Harrison's people knew a good campaign gimmick when it got handed to them on a silver platter. His roots, of course, went deep into buckeye country, and soon log cabins made of buckeye wood were being towed from town to town while supporters sang a ditty that began, "Oh where, tell me, where/ Was your buckeye cabin made?" Harrison's was the first staged political campaign. It not only got him elected, but also spread — and fixed — the image of Ohioan as Buckeye throughout the land.

## *The Buckeye essentials*

State animal — ***white tail deer,*** adopted 1987

State beverage — ***tomato juice,*** adopted with a nod toward Ohio's prodigious crop in 1965

State fossil — the trilobite, ***Isotelus brachycephalus,*** adopted 1985

State gem stone — ***flint,*** perennially favored by Indians for arrowheads, adopted 1965

State herb capital — ***Gahanna,*** designated 1972

State insect — ***ladybug,*** adopted 1975

State official location — ***North Central Great Lakes Region,*** according to U.S. Department of Commerce

State poetry day — ***third Friday of October,*** adopted 1938

State rock song — ***Hang on Sloopy,*** adopted 1985

State wildflower — white trillium, ***Trillium grandiflorum,*** adopted 1986

# The fine points: Advanced Buckeye

### Ohio

has its semantic roots in the Iroquois word *O-he-yo*, meaning "great river," but the first English appearance of the word in a book occurred in 1756 in *A Fourth Letter to the People of England on the Conduct of the M---rs in Alliances, Fleets, and Armies, since the First Differences on the Ohio, to the taking of Minorca by the French*, by John Shebbeare (printed for M. Collier, London).

### The Capital

has a peripatetic history, having been variously located between 1788 and 1816 in Marietta, Cincinnati, Chillicothe, and Zanesville, according to the shifting political requirements of Territory and State, until it found a permanent home in Columbus. ❤

### The Statehouse

took twenty-two years (1839-1861) and $1,359,121.45 to build. Architect Henry Walter of Cincinnati designed the Greek Revival building with Doric columns and foundation walls fifteen feet thick at the corners. The building measures 184-by-304 feet, and the grounds occupy ten square acres in downtown Columbus. Convicts (originally hired at forty cents a day) provided much of the labor for the Statehouse, which Frank Lloyd Wright called "the most honest of state capitols, sincere and forthright."

### Statehood

for all practical purposes was granted on March 1, 1803, when Ohio became the first state carved from the Northwest Territory; however, it was not *officially* admitted to the Union until August 7, 1953. ❤

### The Great Seal

was inspired by a view of the sun rising over Mt. Logan and is replete with symbolism. Designer William Creighton included a sheaf of wheat for Ohio the bountiful; a sheaf of seventeen arrows since Ohio is the seventeenth state; and the sun above the mountains because Ohio was the first state west of the Alleghenies. ♥

♥ As various towns jockeyed to grab the capital brass ring, Ohio's seat of government was moved by the strength of the prevailing political winds. Until, that is, four men from Franklinton offered to give the state ten acres for the capital and "a like amount nearby for a state penitentiary." Franklinton was located on the west bank of the Scioto River, and their gift, located directly across the water, was occupied only by a cabin. *Construction of a Statehouse,* library, and office building began in 1912, and by the time the Ohio government moved there in 1916, the cabin had been replaced by a thriving town of 8,000 with the proud name of Columbus. But even then, the *permanency* of the situation seemed in doubt. When the cornerstone for a the present Statehouse was laid on July 4, 1839, some folks grumbled that its site on the Scioto wasn't healthy or near enough the state's center. Convict labor from the penitentiary was used during construction, and a newspaper of the day commented, "The boys in stripes move pretty briskly for the warm weather. We see that the whole row of the front columns has been put in facing High Street." The foundation with walls twelve-feet thick was set by the first winter, built strong enough to withstand the pressure from malcontents to move the Statehouse elsewhere.

♥ Even though Ohio has been sending Congressmen and Senators to Washington, D.C., since 1803, the U.S. Congress never actually voted on the formal resolution admitting Ohio to the Union. On what would have been the state's true sesquicentennial in 1953, this oversight was corrected when Representative George Bender introduced a bill for **Ohio statehood.** Meanwhile, Rep. Clarence Brown threatened that Ohio was going to apply for foreign aid if the bill didn't pass. But President Eisenhower swiftly signed the measure, noting that he wanted Ohioans to be able to celebrate their 150th birthday legally.

But even today, there are nay-sayers who claim that Ohio still is *not* a state because Congress's *ex post facto* statehood resolution is unconstitutional. Samuel Pearce Holton, the president of a Georgia college, even filed a federal suit to prevent Ohioans from voting in the 1984 election. "The course of history of this country has been changed," he argued, "be it for better or

for worse, by the unlawful votes of the people of the Territory of Ohio, masquerading as a state and sending delegates to Congress to vote, unlawfully, on issues of great importance."

♥ Legend has it that when twenty-one year old **William Creighton** was charged with designing the state seal, he rode out from the temporary capital at Chillicothe to consult his friend, Thomas Worthington, one of Ohio's first two U.S. Senators. Worthington called his fine country estate Adena, a Persian word for paradise. There Creighton got into a card game with some other guests, and they played the night away. When dawn broke, Creighton noticed how the sun climbing behind Mount Logan cast a rosy light on the surrounding wheat fields. "Gentlemen," he declared, "there is our seal."

# Intestinal fortitude

## Great moments in Buckeye gastronomy

*1820* First Ohio cheese factory opens in Champaign County; six people turn 12,500 gallons of milk into $1226 worth of cheese.

*1830's* The dietary theories of **Dr. Sylvester Graham** come to the dining halls of Oberlin College. White bread, wine, and meat "which stimulates sexual excess" are out; fruits, vegetables, and coarse-ground grains to aid digestion are in. Graham crackers sorely test student appetites, and one minister's wife complains, "you can always tell a Grahamite by his lean and hungry look."

*1833* Jacob Ebert, Cadiz, gets the first patent on a soda fountain.

*1864* Georgetown's most famous General, **Ulysses S. Grant,** sustains himself on cucumbers and coffee during the Army of the Potomac's Wilderness Campaign.

*1890* In Cleveland, **Henry Avery** makes the first aluminum saucepan, which Mrs. Avery uses faithfully for forty-three years.

*1900* Conrad Beck of Cleveland, "a specialist on barbecue," is imported to Columbus where butchers toast old soldiers with a big roast — one spring lamb, 3 bullocks, 40 rounds of beef, 300 pounds of pork, and an 800 pound ox. Newspapers report that "bread piled higher than a man's head occupied an entire tent . . ."

*1911* Having received the first patent for hydrogenation, Procter & Gamble markets Crisco, one small step for pie, one giant leap for pan frying.

*1913* In Miamisburg, **Sherwin "Cocky" Porter** pioneers the drive-up window when he starts selling hamburgers out of milk wagon on the town square.

*1924* Carl Rutherford Taylor, Cleveland, invents the ice cream cone rolling machine and helps to fill the national sweet tooth with the first mass cone production.

*1943* Champion gourmand and Franklin County courthouse librarian **Rudy Wittenmeier,** whose finest hour came when he downed nine chickens and twenty-four ears of corn plus bread, butter, and beer at one sitting, announces that he is going on a diet — from seven to three meals per day.

*1956* TAT Restaurant, 3278 East Main, is the first restaurant to serve pizza in Columbus.

*1978* For the first time, blue ribbon food is auctioned at the State Fair; when **Elsie Hack's** apple pie brings $2000, Governor Rhodes predicts, "Next year you're gonna have pies from 11th to 17th Avenues."

*1981* *Food and Wine* announces that Miamisburg is home to one of the top U.S. potato chips, Wagner's.

*1983* Glennburgers selling for 98 cents appear at the launch pad called New Concord, hometown of ex-astronaut **John Glenn** and kickoff point for his latest — soon-to-be-aborted — mission, capturing the White House.

*1985* The brothers of Zeta Beta Tau, Bowling Green State University, build a four mile banana split — the world's longest.

# Eat Ohio

**Food for thought**

World's largest pork rind snack maker: Lima's Rudolph Foods, 70 million pounds per year

Big Cheese: Ohio, number one in U.S. Swiss cheese production, some 56 million pounds in 1989.

Largest Swiss cheese producer: at 30 million pounds per year, Brewster Dairy leads the U.S.

World class popcorn: Prairie Maize Co., Morral, at 20 million pounds per year, the No. 1 unpopped popcorn exporter

"Chicken Capital of the World" — Barberton, serving up five tons of chicken per week

World's longest bar: 405.6 foot behemoth at the Beer Barrel Saloon, South Bass Island

Chickened out: Ohio, first state to require precise labeling on poultry cuts

5th and Broad: Columbus site of the first Wendy's restaurant, opened November, 1969, still hot and juicy after all these years

The fruitcake abideth: in November, 1878, Fridelia Ford baked her last rum fruitcake in her Lucas County farmhouse. After she died, her family preserved her spirit and her fruitcake by passing it from generation to generation. One man taking the cake was a great-grandson who says the cake was last sampled some decades ago by an uncle. "We like to say that he lived for two years more," allowed Morgan Ford, "so it couldn't have been too bad ..."

# *Our favorite sobriquets*

### By their nicknames we shall know them

"Heartland of the Nation"; "Mother of Presidents" — **Ohio**

"Rubber City of the World"; "Home of the Soap Box Derby"; "Capital of West Virginia" — **Akron**

"Gem City"; "Birthplace of Aviation"; "High School Reunion Capital of the U.S." — **Dayton**

"Queen City of the West"; "City of Seven Hills"; "Paris of America;" "Porkopolis"; "Blue Chip City" — **Cincinnati**

"Information Capital of the World" — **Columbus**

"Rock 'n' Roll Capital of the World"; "Best Location in the Nation"; "Pierogi Capital of America"; "Chitterlings Capital of the North" — **Cleveland**

"Clay Center of the World" — **Urichsville**

"Earthquake Capital of Ohio" — **Anna**

"City of Champions" — **Massillon,** of high school football fame

"The King" — **Clark Gable**

"Saint's Rest" — **New Concord,** Muskingum County bastion of Presbyterianism

"One Mile Long and Three Blocks Wide" — **Pomeroy**

"Y-Bridge City" — **Zanesville**

"Yale of the West" — **Western Reserve College,** now Case Western Reserve University

126

"Mother of Fraternities"; "Cradle of Coaches" — *Miami University*

"The Red Napoleon" — *Tecumseh*

"Calico Charlie" — Ohio *Governor Charles Foster,* who ran a general store instead of soldiering during the Civil War

"Liberator of Bulgaria" — New Lexington newspaperman and freedom fighter *J. S.MacGahan*

"Little Miss Sure Shot" — *Annie Oakley*

"Cump" — Civil War *General William Tecumseh Sherman*

"Drummer Boy of Shiloh" — *Johnny Clem* of Newark

"Father of American Education" — *Horace Mann,* first president of Antioch College

"Father of Human Genetics" — Ohio State University medical school professor *Laurence H. Snyder*

"His Fradulency" — *Benjamin Harrison,* after he squeaked into the White House

"Old Iron Pants" — *General Curtis LeMay* of Columbus

"King of the Cowboys" — Portsmouth-born *Roy Rogers*

"Mr. Clean"; "Old Magnet Tail"; "First American in Earth Orbit" — Marine pilot, astronaut, and U.S. Senator *John Glenn*

# Ladies of the club

## Women of means, manners, and method

### Florence Ellinwood Allen

She was the most celebrated woman jurist of her day — the first elected female judge in the U.S. (Cuyahoga County Common Pleas Court, 1920), the first elected to a state supreme court (Ohio, 1922), the first appointed to a U.S. Court of Appeals (1934), and the first woman to sentence a man to death (Frank Motto, electrocuted 1921).

### Alice Pike Barney

Cincinnati-born artiste, bon vivant, and blithe spirit. ❤

### Mother Bickerdyke

Born on a Knox County farm in 1817, Mary Ann Ball Bickerdyke became the nation's first war nurse, ministering to wounded Union soldiers on the western front. Her courage under enemy fire drew the admiration of Generals Grant and Sherman, but her compassion earned her the enlisted men's tribute, "Mother." When a hospital ran short of food, she refortified the troops with luck and pluck and a strong jaw-boning attack on farmers, returning with her "cow and hen army" of 1,100 reluctant enlistees. After the war, Mother Bickerdyke took part in a victory parade in Washington. It is said that when she rode by on her familiar white horse, she got as much applause as General Sherman.

### Dr. Elizabeth Blackwell

In 1849, this former Cincinnatian became the first woman in the U.S. to be graduated from medical school — after her applications had been rejected twenty-nine times.

### Mary Catherine Campbell

In 1922, with a thirty-inch bosom, she became the first Miss America. When the Columbus woman took the title again in 1923, she also became the second and the only two-time winner in history.

### Martha Kinney Cooper

As the wife of Governor Myers Y. Cooper, this Cincinnatian founded the Ohioana Library Association, the only archive in the U.S. charged with fostering the arts of a particular state. Her $10,000 endowment parlayed what began in 1929 as a modest acquisition for the governor's mansion into a collection of more than 30,000 books and 4000 pieces of sheet music.

### Louise Atcherson Curtis

At the appointment of President Warren G. Harding in 1922, this Columbusite became the first woman to serve in the U.S. Foreign Service; she was legation secretary in Switzerland until 1924.

### Mrs. Joseph Dennewitz

A Chillicothe resident, she was Ohio's only triple Gold Star mother; her sons John, James, and William were all killed within a year of each other during World War II.

### Hessie Donahue

She was known as the woman who knocked out John L. Sullivan, accidentally, of course, but the housewife in bloomers gave the champ a right that put him out cold. Hessie, who came from Cleveland, warmed up the crowds by sparring with the Great John L. at boxing exhibitions. One night in March, 1892, he made her mad, and Hessie landed her lucky punch. She got so much publicity that John L. made her "knockout" a regular part of his act and paid her $15 a night.

### Catherine Ewing

This schoolteacher founded at Marietta in 1867, the world's first public orphanage. "Aunt Katie Fay" paid for faculty out of her own pocket and worked tirelessly for the Ohio legislation that established children's homes in every county.

### Harriet Clark McCabe

This Delaware lady gave the Woman's Christian Temperance Union its name, drafted its constitution in 1874, and was the organization's first Ohio president.

### Jerrie Mock

The "flying housewife" from Columbus became the first woman to solo an airplane around world — in thirty days, in 1964. She is also the first American to receive the Louis Bleriot aviation medal.

### Non-Hel-E-Ma

Chief of Grenadier Squaw Town near Circleville, she helped her brother Cornstalk lead a thousand Shawnee in the attack on Lord Dunmore's forces at Point Pleasant. Many consider this 1774 battle to be the first one of the American Revolution, for Virginia Governor Dunmore's foray was in protest of the English Quebec Act, which prohibited white settlement in the Ohio Valley. The Indians' defeat brought a stream of whites pouring across the Appalachians.

### Annie Oakley

She was a superstar. The dark-haired little girl who started out bagging game in Darke County ended up performing for Queen Victoria and shooting a cigarette from between the confident lips of Kaiser Wilhelm. But for all the acclaim that Buffalo Bill Cody's Wild West Show brought her in the 1880's, "Little Miss Sure Shot" never succumbed to the demons of fame. She kept her dignity, her marriage, and her reputation intact. And she controlled her aim to the point of insisting that her burial gown be hemmed to the proper length.

### Sally Jane Priesand

When she was ordained in 1972 at Cincinnati's Hebrew Union College-Jewish Institute of Religion, this Clevelander became the first woman rabbi in the U.S.

### Judith A. Resnick

An Akron native and one of the first women astronauts, she died in the space shuttle *Challenger* explosion, January 28, 1986.

### Susanna Madora Salter

At the age of 27, this Belmont County native became the first woman mayor in the U.S. (and an international celebrity) when the voters of Argonia, Kansas, elected her on April 4, 1887, by a two-thirds majority.

### Lucy Sessions

She was the first Black woman in the U.S. to earn a college degree — from Oberlin, in 1850.

### The Schwarz Sisters

The Misses Jo and Hermene began giving ballet lessons in Dayton in 1927. A modest beginning, perhaps, but since then their Schwarz School for the Dance and Experimental Group for Young Dancers — which later became the Dayton Ballet — have earned a national reputation for exquisitely trained dancers, many of them principals with the American and Joffre ballets.

### Gloria Steinem

A native of Toledo, she is the co-founder of *Ms.* Magazine and one of the most visible leaders of the Feminist Movement.

### Lucy Stone

She worked her way through Oberlin College (Class of 1847) because her father thought educating a woman was a waste of money. A suffragette and abolitionist, she was the inspiration for the Lucy Stone League, whose members refused to take their husband's last names.

### Victoria Claflin Woodhull

Her priorities began and ended with her overwhelming sense of her own best interests, which neatly explains how an itinerant Ohio spiritualist became the first woman U.S. presidential candidate (1872); an unabashed advocate of women's rights, Free Love, and legalized prostitution; a newspaper publisher who printed the first English translation of the *Communist Manifesto*; a New York stockbroker; the first woman to speak before a Congressional committee; a close friend of Cornelius Vanderbilt; and, finally, a wealthy dowager who died (sitting up) on her English estate. Perhaps being born in Homer had foreshadowed her entire life, which took on, after all, epic proportions. But Victoria always had been fond of the Greeks. She often said that her spirit was under the control of Demosthenes, who *also* had remarkable powers of persuasion.

### Katharine Wright

On the 25th anniversary of the first airplane flight, someone wrote, "There would have been no Kitty Hawk without Kitty Wright." She taught Latin in a Dayton high school, but to her brothers Orville and Wilbur, she was confidante, counselor, hostess, nurse, press agent, cook, official correspondent, and their indefatigable cheerleader. When Wilbur took her on her first flight in 1909, she tied a rope around her legs to hold her skirt down, and when she died twenty years later, planes from the airfield that is now Wright-Patterson Air Force Base dropped flowers on her grave.

♥ Wealth and privilege were not uncommon birthrights for children born to Cincinnati's enterprising families during the mid-1800's. But *Alice Pike Barney* received from her father the more precious heritage of culture. Samuel N. Pike, "a self-made man of exquisite taste," built the Cincinnati's first opera house and the Grand Opera House in New York City. For his handsome daughter, lessons in voice and dance were *de rigueur*, and Alice thrived in an atmosphere of "genteel bohemianism." When Pike entertained, the opera house stars he invited were often outshined by the ebullient daughter who acted as his hostess.

On her first trip to Europe, Alice got herself engaged to Sir Henry Morton Stanley, the famous soldier-journalist who had presumed to find Dr. Livingston at Lake Tanganyika. Though Stanley named his Congo exploration boat *Lady Alice*, she suddenly jilted him to marry Albert Clifford Barney of Dayton. The Barney family had made a fortune manufacturing railroad cars during the Civil War, and Albert supported Alice and their two daughters grandly as they alternated between Cincinnati, New York, and Europe. Eventually he built them a mansion in Washington, D.C., where the family moved in 1888.

Alice took to studying painting in France. She sought out the finest teachers, among them James McNeil Whistler, who became her close friend. Her portrait of daughter Natalie was accepted by the Salon in Paris, and she held a one-woman show at Washington's Corcoran Gallery.

After Paris, Alice found Washington pale indeed. "What is capital life after all?" she wrote. "Small talk and lots to eat, and infinite series of teas and dinners. Art? There is none."

Having found a cultural vacuum, Alice determined to fill it. Early in 1902, she commissioned an architect to build her a mansion on Massachusetts Avenue. It was to be not only her home, but also her salon. Ever-proper Albert, who had always kept a check-rein on her high spirits, died, thus leaving her free to fill the mansion with artists, friends, paintings, and elaborate furnishings. Across the musician's balcony, she stenciled a passage from Goethe: "The highest problem of art is to create the illusion of a higher reality."

Between entertainments, Alice painted; wrote and produced her own plays; designed the costumes for Anna Palova's one-act ballet of 1915; and helped start the first federal outdoor theater, the Sylvan Theatre, on the grounds of the Washington Monument. She also wed Christian Dominique Hemmick, an actor in her play *Moon Man*. Alice likened him to a Greek god, but he proved a tarnished one who shared her affinity for handsome young men. She announced the end of their December-May liaison by cutting the "Mr." off her party invitations.

Alice died, fittingly, at a concert, and is buried in Dayton. Her headstone reads, "Alice Pike Barney, the Talented One." She left a fine art collection, her own notable paintings, and Barney Studio House, which is now part of the Smithsonian Institution.

# Ohio geology

## A garden of our earthy delights

### Anna's Fault

Since 1875, more than forty earthquakes have originated near the Shelby County village of Anna, including one on March 9, 1937, that was the worst quake (approximately 5.5 on the Richter scale) with an Ohio epicenter ever recorded. The citizens of Anna are subject to falling chimneys and twisted pipe organs because of the village's double trouble location above both a fault and the drift-filled bed of the prehistoric Teays River. Sediments magnify motion, so when the fault quakes, Anna, quite literally, shakes.

### Berea Grit

Alias Berea sandstone, Ohio stone, Cleveland stone, and Independence stone, this cache of light sandstone in the Western Reserve not only made Berea the grindstone capital of the world in the 1800's, but also provided Ohio with some of its firmest foundations — including homes, courthouses, college buildings, the Garfield Memorial, and the Soldiers' and Sailors' Monument and Hope Memorial Bridge in Cleveland.

### Blue Hole of Castalia

It is probably the only artesian well in the world with its own address, 502 North Washington Street, Castalia, Erie County, Ohio. At least forty-five feet deep, the Hole is so well fed by an underground river that the 7519 gallons which flow through every minute could supply a city of 75,000. The water is an even 48° and dead — totally without the oxygen that sustains fish.

### Buckeye Lake Cranberry Bog

This is a wee bit o' Canada in Licking County, where glaciers formed a swamp in which cold-loving northern flora thrive. Several thousand years old and barely holding out against erosion and

Evinrude, Cranberry Island is an Ohio orginal —
the only island *cum* cranberry bog in the world.

### Flint Ridge

Nine thousand years ago, Indians from across
the continent already prized the red, blue, green,
yellow, and pink flint that abounds in southeastern
Licking and northwest Muskingum County. Elsewhere in Ohio, the flint is typically black or white,
but elsewhere wasn't covered by a fortuitous sea
300 million years ago. Though white men today
call this bonanza Vanport flint and seek it out for
jewelry, the shallow quarries where the Indians
dug are still visible on the ridge.

### Glacial grooves

Between one and two million years ago,
glaciers repeatedly advanced and retreated over
all but the southeastern part of the state. The
mountains of ice didn't leave completely until only
about fourteen thousand years ago, and of course,
anything that big couldn't go away without leaving
a calling card of sorts — erratics, moraines,
kames, and the scarred rock that we call glacial
grooves. Today the north shore of Kelleys Island
displays the largest and most outstanding glacial
gooves known to man — deep trails etched in
the limestone by the farewell performance of the
Wisconsinan behemoths.

### Mammoths

Common during the Ice Age, fossil remains
of more than fifty of these grassland mammals —
extinct for 10,000 years — have been found in
the state.

### Mastodons

Even more common than mammoths during
the Ice Age, fossil remains of about 150 of these

mammals have been found in the state, where they roamed the unglaciated southeast and fed in spruce forests; they, too, have been extinct for ten millennia.

### Meteorites

Perhaps the rarest rocks in Ohio. Aside from the meteorites believed to have been imported from Kansas by Indians of the Hopewell culture, there have been only five meteorite "finds" (unwitnessed landing) and two "falls" (witnessed). The finds occurred in Clark, Hamilton, Montgomery, Preble, and Wayne Counties. The falls were witnessed on February 13, 1893, when a 1.98 pound meteorite came in from the Deep Cold near Pricetown, Highland County, and on May 1, 1860, when more than thirty fragments of a large meteorite fell near New Concord. ❤

### Rock of the Ages

The biggest rock ever found in Ohio is the Brassfield erratic, a 430 million year old mass of limestone from five to seventeen feet thick that covers most of an acre. It was left by glaciers near the north fork of Olive Branch not far from Oregonia. In the 1840's, erratics were thought to be remnants of the Biblical Flood, but they are merely rocks that have been picked up and carried (by natural forces) from one spot to another.

### Salt

Ohio has enough halite to supply the U.S. for the next 32,000 years. Formed from sea water 400 million years ago, the primary deposits are mined from tunnels 2000 feet below Lake Erie or extracted via brine mines in northern Ohio. An average of 26 million tons is produced annually — forty percent of which goes to industry, thirty-five percent on roads, and five percent into America's salt shakers.

♥ The *New Concord meteorite* made one of the grandest entrances ever recorded in Ohio. A thunderous roar lasting about thirty seconds alerted citizens in two counties to the bright fireball that was racing across the noon sky. In the earth's atmosphere, the meteorite split up into fiery fragments that scattered across thirty square miles. One of them struck and killed the day's only casualty — a calf. Folks picked up the pieces and found that all together they weighed 500 pounds. There probably still are undiscovered fragments of the meteorite around New Concord, but the largest one recovered (103 pounds) is owned by the Department of Geology at Marietta College.

# Those magnificent men

## A few brief shining moments in Dayton

**1903** The Dog That Didn't Bark

When Orville and Wilbur Wright telegraph home to Hawthorn Street telling of their first successful flight on December 17 at Kittyhawk, a Dayton city editor is wary of Wrights bearing news. "Fifty-seven seconds?" he says. "If it had been fifty-seven minutes it *might* have been a news item." After showing brother Lorin the door, he runs the headline that the **Wright Brothers** are expected home for Christmas, thereby becoming editor of the greatest story never told, a position he holds until 1908 when scooped by the New York and London papers.

Orville and Wilbur *do* get back for Christmas, thereby becoming the First Airplane Pilots to come home for the holidays.

**1905** First Fuel-Emergency Landing

Dayton's most famous sons may have gone to the windy shores of North Carolina for their first flight, but they always said that **Huffman Prairie** in Dayton was where they learned *how* to fly. The cow pasture makes a dandy place for the Wright Brothers to perfect the techniques of flying. Between June and October, they practice circles and figure-eights to the delight of nearby farmers and traction passengers whose heads are constantly turned upward by the spectacle of men flying. On one of their last test-flights, they keep the *Flyer* airborne for an astounding thirty-eight minutes and three seconds. Later, the usually meticulous brothers allow that they could have stayed up even longer, but forgot to fill the gas tank.

**1909** Katharine Wright Inspires the Hobble Skirt

In France as the "social manager" to her widely-acclaimed brothers, **Katharine Wright** gets at Pau on February 15, her first aeroplane ride.

For modesty's sake, Dayton's First Lady of Flight ties a rope around her legs to hold her skirts in place, then goes aloft with Wilbur for a thrilling seven minutes and four seconds.

**1910** The Fabric of Legend

On November 7, the Wright B Flyer takes off from Dayton's Huffman Prairie with the *First Cargo Flight*, a bolt of rose silk and several other silk pieces, all of which weigh more than a hundred pounds. The destination is Columbus, and at take-off, pilot Philip Parmalee tells Orville Wright that he doesn't know the way, whereupon Orville hands him a road map and tells him to wing it. Orville also provides a sack lunch, which is the *First Known In-Flight Meal.* With his silken cargo strapped in the passenger seat, Parmalee, who had declined to take-off and land on department store roofs, reaches Columbus in sixty-three minutes. He circles the Ohio State Penitentiary and then lands at the Driving Park. Max Morehouse, the Columbus merchant who paid the $5000 tab for Parmalee's flight and subsequent air show, cashes in by selling the bolt by the yard and the silkpieces as tiny scraps stuck on souvenir postcards.

**1911** First Minor Passengers

Orville Wright takes the first children up in an airplane — his nephew *Ellwyn* and nieces *Leontine* and *Ivonette.* Ivonette, wearing a student pilot's leather jacket and gloves, goes last. As they circle, Uncle Orv notices the Springfield trolley heading for Simms Station. "Shall we race?" he asks, and Ivonette agrees. They fly along, and Uncle Orv and the traction glide to a stop at the same time.

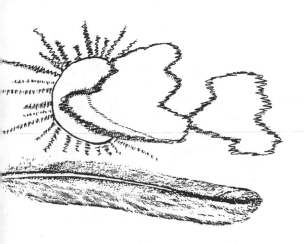

**1918** A Lightning "Bug"

On October 2 (too late for World War I, too soon for World War II), Dayton's resident wizard, Charles F. "Boss" Kettering, tests the *First Guided Missile,* a 300-pound airplane with fifteen-foot detachable wings. The rail-launched Kettering Aerial Torpedo reminds folks of a bug, and it carries a deadly sting — hundreds of pounds of explosives that hone-in on targets at fifty miles per hour. Kettering's tests are so impressive that the government orders two thousand, but the war ends before the missiles can be used.

**1927** Lucky Lindy, Unlucky Lawn

After Lindbergh flew the Atlantic in May, he flew to Dayton in June to pay homage to Orville, the surviving Wright brother. A throng of curiosity seekers storm the Wright home, *Hawthorn Hill.* They climb trees, stampede the shrubbery, and mill about the portico demanding to see the new hero of the air. As a kindness to the flora, Orville and Lindbergh quiet the multitude by appearing on a front balcony. Then they retreat inside, where Lindbergh spends a peaceable night in the bedroom that had been intended for Wilbur.

**1919** A Happy Landing

After the first practical parachute is invented by Floyd Smith at Wright Field, Lt. Harold R. Harris makes the *First Emergency Parachute Jump* on October 20. Bailing out of his crippled airplane at 2500 feet, the future brigadier general lands in a grape arbor on the north side of town.

**1920** First to Fly the Stratosphere . . . and Return

On Feb. 27, McCook Field test pilot Rudolph "Shorty" Schroeder sets a *world altitude record* of 33,113 feet when he flies a LePere biplane into the stratosphere. In the open cockpit with only an oxygen mask and goggles for protection, Major Schroeder climbs for nearly two hours into temperatures of minus forty-five degrees. When he lifts his goggles to read some instruments, his eyeballs freeze and blind him. "In less than a minute," reported a Dayton newspaper," all became black before him, He described the sensation as an explosion having taken place in his head . . ." The major passes out, and his plane goes into a dive. When he comes to, Schroeder is only a few thousand feet above the ground. As his plane plummeted toward the earth, the ice had cracked and cut his eyeballs, but Schroeder manages to make out Wright Field, where, says the newspaper, he "landed without mishap."

### 1946 On the Hot Seat

After the *panic rack* is developed at Wright Field, Sgt. Larry Lambert becomes the First Person to Use an Ejection Seat, punching out of a P-61 at nearly 8000 feet.

# Natural wonders

### Delia Corbly Martin

was a child on her way to church when Indians attacked, scalped her, and left her for dead. Although wounds covered the entire crown of her head, she survived to marry Miami County pioneer Levi Martin and bear him ten children. Mrs. Martin, who blamed the loathsome and cronic headaches she suffered on the scalping, protected her head by training her remaining hair to grow up and over the wounds. She died in 1836, forty-two years after the attack.

### John Chapman

who is best known as the itinerant planter Johnny Appleseed, went barefoot on his appointed frontier rounds, a habit which made his heels and soles legendary. According to a Mansfield reporter, his feet were "dark, hard, and horny, calloused so heavily as to resemble the hide of an elephant. Sometimes he showed off a trifle by thrusting pins into his feet without causing a bodily tremor. If they were cut, or opened by a sore, Johnny would call upon the mistress of a nearby dwelling to borrow her red-hot iron, and then would immediately sear the wound closed, to her utmost horror."

### Plymouth Rock Hen

belonging to Dwight Maugins laid inside out eggs. According to the *Springfield Daily News* of April 10, 1906, "The outside covering of the remarkable product of this extraordinary hen is the thin white skin usually found just under the shell. The white of the egg comes next, then comes the regulation shell, surrounding the yolk."

### Tom Jones

was the original giant in P. T. Barnum's circus. "Long Tom" was seven feet four and a half inches tall when he enlisted in the Fifty-first Ohio Volunteers during the Civil War. Shot through the neck during a skirmish, a fellow soldier saved his life by stopping the blood with a postage stamp, which he carried absorbed in his body to his grave. With Barnum, he appeared before Queen Victoria and played a towering Uncle Sam at William McKinley's home in Canton. Mr. Jones retired to a farm in his hometown of Newark, where he died in 1909 at age 71.

### Noah Orr

was also a Barnum discovery, but the awesome — seven feet eight inches tall, 550 pounds — farmhand from Sodom soon capitalized on his own assets. The "Union County Giant" founded the Lilliputian Company, starring himself and a gaggle of midgets in *Jack the Giant Killer.*

### Fanny Mills

was the Sandusky farm girl who had the biggest feet in the world, which in 1882 were investigated closely by a *Cincinnati Enquirer* reporter: "Your correspondent undertook the delicate task of measuring the huge masses of flesh called feet. The right foot is one foot six inches in length, and the left one inch shorter. Over the instep of the right foot is twenty-one inches, and over the other one inch less. The big toe of the left foot is eleven inches in circumference. The right foot is longer than the left by an inch, but the latter is heavier and thicker. The feet are respectively seven and eight inches wide." ❤

### Anna Swan and Martin Van Buren Bates

were a couple of giants (seven feet eleven inches and 413 pounds and seven feet nine inches and 470 pounds respectively) who repaired to the peace and quiet of Seville in 1873 after years of touring with P. T. Barnum and his Greatest Show on Earth. They became known about town not so much for their size as its effects — the house with doorways ten feet high, a dance floor that caved in under their weight, and their broadening influence on the Baptists, who had to widen a church pew so they could sit together.

### Stanley Radwan

the Polish-born strongman of Cleveland performed such feats as holding six men in the air with one arm, snapping iron chains, tearing quarters in half, and most remarkably, surviving a German concentration camp, where, it is said, he defied Hitler in person by collapsing a revolver barrel with his teeth.

### Dougie and Debbie Schee

are the twins who were born nearly seven weeks apart in Delaware, 1955.

### Vernon Craig

in the 1970's set a world's record for lying on a bed of nails — twenty-five hours and twenty minutes while holding 1642 pounds on his chest. Also a fire-walker, the Wooster man took a comparable record for enduring the hottest coals — 1494°F, set August 14, 1976, at the International Festival of Yoga and Esoteric Sciences.

### William Milligan

was found not guilty by reason of insanity in a 1978 Columbus rape case when it was discovered that his multiple personality had numerous separate identities, among them a three-year-old girl and an Englishman.

♥ Fanny Mills was afflicted with elephantiasis, but her mother always blamed her deformity on Fanny's father, who had forced the woman to wash a horse's swollen leg when she was pregnant. Fanny wore pillowcases for socks, and her specially-made size 30 shoes cost fifty-five dollars per pair. She gained fame in 1885 by appearing at a Philadelphia museum. A poster replete with bad jokes and worse puns ("no person ever had so much understanding; the old woman who lived in a shoe could have rented apartments . . .") attracted a passel of suitors with the announcement that her father would give $5000 and a farm to any respectable man who would marry Fanny. One South Carolinian "with a liberality so characteristic of Southern chivalry" wanted her to send him money for the trip to Ohio, while a New Jersey man wrote that he neither smoke nor drank and in his entire life had only once been out past ten p.m. — when his mother's house burned down and he had to climb out a second-story window. In truth, Fanny's dairy farmer father was dead, and she had consented to exhibit herself only to help support her mother. Blonde and petite above the hips, Fanny was not without her charms, however, and she married the brother of her chaperone, William L. Brown. They settled into domesticity on Perkins Avenue in Sandusky, where Fanny lived until an abcess caused her death at age 39 in 1899.

# The body politic

### The facts of Ohio's political life

**Slimmest gubernatorial victory**
1848, when Seabury Ford shoos in past John Weller by 311 votes

**Largest gubernatorial landslide**
1966, James Rhodes defeats Frazier Reams, Jr., by 703,223 votes

**First Black man elected to office in the United States**
John Mercer Langston, elected Clerk of Brownhelm Township, Lorain County, 1854

**First Black Ohio Congressman**
Louis Stokes of Cleveland, elected November, 1968

**First Black Mayor in Ohio**
Robert C. Henry, who in 1967 took office in Springfield

**First Black Mayor of a major U.S. city**
Carl Burton Stokes, the great-grandson of a slave, who in 1968 won Cleveland's mayorality over Seth Taft, the great-grandson of President Taft

**First mother and son simultaneously elected to U.S. Congress**
Cleveland's Frances Payne Bolton and son Oliver Payne Bolton, 1952

**First woman elected to State office**
Gertrude W. Donahey, a Democrat form Tuscarawas County, elected State Treasurer, 1970

### Only father to succeed his son as governor

Mordecai Bartley, who in 1844, followed Thomas Welles Bartley, the Speaker of the Ohio Senate, who became acting governor upon Wilson Shannon's resignation

### Only father and son simulataneously elected to the Ohio House of Representatives

Democrats Robert E. Hagan (father) of Madison and Robert F. Hagan (son) of Youngstown, sworn in together in 1987

### Youngest Ohio Governor

Thomas Bartley, age 32, who served from April 15 to December 3, 1844

### Youngest person elected to Ohio State House

Twenty-one-year-old Representative Sherrod Brown, a Mansfield Democrat

### Salmon P. Chase, Cincinnati

Although he abandoned the pulpit for the law, his ingrained sense of right and wrong made him one of the nation's most outspoken and visible Abolitionists. His stance on slavery probably cost Chase the Presidential nomination he so deeply coveted, but he served admirably as Governor of Ohio (1856-1860) and was twice-elected U.S. Senator (1849 and 1861). Perhaps his finest hour came when President Lincoln appointed him Secretary of the Treasury in 1861. In the midst of Civil War turmoil and uncertainty, Chase accomplished the crucial task of not only organizing a national banking system, but also of inspiring public confidence in it. He served as Chief Justice of the Supreme Court during the wrenching Reconstruction era, and his unwavering support of suffrage earned him the sobriquet, "Attorney General of the Negroes," a people who in turn gratefully presented him with a silver pitcher for "public service on behalf of the oppressed."

### Thomas Corwin, Lebanon

He was a public servant extraordinaire — Prosecuting Attorney of Warren County (1818-28), State Legislator (1821-23; 1829-30), Governor of Ohio (1840-42), a five-term U.S. Congressman, Senator (1845-50), and Secretary of the Treasury (1850-1853). A loyal Whig who tirelessly supported William Henry Harrison's bid for the Presidency, Corwin was a man of wit and eloquence who in 1847 delivered an impassioned speech in the U.S. Senate denouncing the Mexican War as an act of conquest. "If I were a Mexican," Corwin told his fellow Senators, "I would ask you, 'Have you not room enough in your own country to bury your dead?'" His position was vindicated in 1861, when President Lincoln appointed him Minister to Mexico. Corwin, who died in 1865, once suggested that his tombstone should read, "Dearly beloved by his family; universally despised by Democrats; useful in life only to knaves and pretended friends."

## George B. Cox, *Cincinnati*

He was the "Boss" in the grand old tradition of city political machines. From 1888 to 1910, observed the *Cincinnati Enquirer*, "no man had a chance to get on the Republican ticket without the approval of Cox"; his organization was "in its way, more complete, more exacting, and under more rigid discipline, than Tammany Hall." Actually, Cox had been to New York for some instruction at Tammany Hall, not that he particularly needed it. Though Cox was only elected to one public office (Cincinnati City Council, 1877), he held such an iron-clad grip on the city's politics that by 1905, twenty-three of the twenty-four ward captains he appointed were on a Cincinnati or Hamilton County payrolls. The reform movement bloomed later in Ohio than in the rest of the nation, and the stories of Cox's corruption are legion. It was said that if someone had announced "Your saloon is on fire!" to the City Council, every member would have dashed out. But in all fairness, Cox did provide a sorely needed element of stability in a rapidly growing city where political factions, emerging suburbs, and new public utility, transportation, and communication systems were creating chaos. In 1911, Cox told a New York newspaper, "I had no ambition to become a boss when I entered politics . . . But because of my peculiar fitness, I became boss." And of his foiled enemies, Cox generously said, "Their failings were born in them, and they should not be blamed too much."

### Marcus Alonzo Hanna, *Cleveland*

After he got William McKinley nominated for President at the Republican Convention in 1896, Hanna went home to Cleveland where a jubilant crowd waited at the train station to cheer his triumph. Hanna jokingly thumped his chest as he shouted to a friend, "Big Injun, Me big Injun." Indeed he was, the biggest Chief of them all, the Boss of Bosses, the Kingmaker, the savvy millionaire industrialist who bankrolled McKinley to the White House by putting the touch on his corporate friends, and probably the only man in the country powerful enough to tell Henry Cabot Lodge to go to hell and get away with it. "The businessman in politics," said William Allen White, "was Hanna's American invention." Hanna, convinced that what was good for business was good for America, determined to proselytize that belief by putting "his boy" in the White House, and when he found McKinley, he found the perfect vehicle for his purposes. McKinley, said White, had "a statesman's face, unwrinkled and unperturbed; a face without vision but without guile . . . He walked among men like a bronze statue . . . determinedly looking for his pedestal." Hanna provided that pedestal courtesy of a campaign fund conservatively estimated at $3,500,000, which bought speechwriters, speakers, and 300 tons of McKinley propaganda. All Hanna wanted in return was an appointment to the most exclusive club in the world, the U.S. Senate. McKinley, of course, obliged, though he did so at the expense of the incumbent, the faithful public servant John Sherman, who was thrown the sop of being a token Secretary of State. Hanna thoroughly enjoyed himself as Senator. He reportedly — and fittingly — got more mail than the President, and his offices were known as the "little White House." When the Constitution forced him to actually run for his Senate seat in 1897, Hanna's money greased his way again through probably the dirtiest campaign in Ohio history. "Columbus, Ohio," wrote Hanna biographer Herbert Croly, "came to resemble a medieval city given over to an angry feud between armed partisans . . . Blows were exhanged in the hotels and on the streets, There were threats of assassinations." Though political cartoons pictured Hanna covered in dollar signs and editorials decried bribery and corruption, Hanna was elected, and the scenario that he would succeed McKinley as President seemed written in stone. However, McKinley was felled by an assassin's bullet, and the White House came to be occupied not by McKinley's mentor, but by his Constitutional successor, Theodore Roosevelt. "Now look," said Hanna, "that damned cowboy is President of the United States." It was a blow from which Hanna never recovered. His health deteriorated, and on February 15, 1904 — less than three years after McKinley's assassination — he died.

### Stephen M. Young, *Cleveland*

Foes called him brash and acerbic; friends called him outspoken and independent; nobody ever called him dull. A liberal Democrat, millionaire lawyer, and friend of organized labor, Young served three terms as a U.S. Congressman and was Senator from 1958 to 1970. Both of his Senate victories were upsets, defeating conservative "right-to-work" John Bricker and Robert Taft, Jr. with the ultimate Republican last name. Crusty and not known for mincing words, Young helped derail John Glenn's run for the Democrat's Senate nomination by pointing out that all astronaut Glenn had ever proved was that he could go around the earth in the fetal position. Young considered his vote for the 1963 Limited Test Ban Treaty the most important of his career, but his colorful responses to Ohio constituents' letters made him legendary. To one critic he wrote, "Some idiot has sent me a telegram to which he has affixed your signature." And to the man who wanted the same free transportation for his horse as had been accorded Pakistan's equine gift to Jacqueline Kennedy, Young replied:

"Dear Sir. Acknowledging the letter wherein you insult the wife of our President. Am wondering why you need a horse when there is already one jackass at your address."

# Picture Credits

Pages 68-69: posters from the Cincinnati Historical Society.

Page 72: Taft, from the Hayes Presidential Center. Harding, Library of Congress.

Pages 74-75: McKinley, from the McKinley Museum. Others from the Library of Congress.

Page 77: Harrison, from the Hayes Presidential Center. Grant, Library of Congress.

Page 78: Hayes Presidential Center.

Page 79: Library of Congress.

Page 80: Library of Congress.

Page 81: McKinley Museum.

Page 84: U.S. Department of Interior.

Page 85: Library of Congress.

Page 86: U.S. Department of Interior.

Page 87: Garfield home, Library of Congress; Harrison, Cincinnati Historical Society; McKinley houses, McKinley Museum; Grant, Library of Congress.

Page 89: McKinley Museum.

Page 91: Library of Congress.

Pages 92-93: McKinley Museum.

Page 95. Hayes Presidential Center.

# Index

Adams County 59
Adams, John Quincy 90
Adelphi, Ohio 16
Agricultural Research and
    Development Center
    46
Ai, Ohio 64
airplane 48
Akron, Ohio 16, 19, 29, 47,
    48, 50, 98, 99, 104, 109,
    110, 126, 131
Albrecht Grocery Co. 99
Allen, Lee 54
Allen, Florence Ellinwood
    128
Allen County 58
aluminum extraction 49
aluminum saucepan 122
Amsterdam, Ohio 59
Anderson, Sherwood 16,
    54
Anna, Ohio 126, 136
Ansonia, Ohio 49
Antioch College 127
Arcanum, Ohio 64
Arlington National Ceme-
    tery 85
Armstrong, Neil 101, 108
artificial fish bait 48
Asher, Asher 45
Ashland County 35
Ashtabula County 113
Athens, Ohio 24, 35, 38, 59
Athens County 59
Atwater, Caleb 107
Audubon, John James 16
automatic traffic signal 48
automobile self-starter 48
Avery, Henry 122

B.F. Goodrich 19
Balsley, John 50
Barber, Ohio Columbus 48
Barberton, Ohio 48
Barney, Alice Pike 128, 133-
    135

Barnum, P.T. 146, 147, 148
Bart (the dog) 111
Baskin, John 54, 107
Bates, Anna Swan 147
Bates, Martin Van Buren
    147
Battle of Lake Erie 100
Beard, Daniel Carter 38
Beavercreek, Ohio 39
Beck, Conrad 122
Beckjord, Walt 109
Beene, Geoffrey 38
beer can 48
bees 44
Belfast, Ohio 58
Bellefontaine, Ohio 25, 35
Belmont County 131
Benjamin Harrison Liter-
    ary Society 38
Bennett, John Leon 48
Bensinger, William 26, 27
Berea Grit 136
Berlin, Ohio 59
Bernhardt, Sarah 21
Berry, Stanley 46
Bethel, Ohio 111
Bickerdyke, Mary Ann
    "Mother" 128
bicycle 48
Blackfork, Ohio 29
Blackwell, Dr. Elizabeth
    128
Blue Hole, The 136
book matches 48
Bowling Green, Ohio 38,
    98
Bowling Green State Uni-
    versity 123
Boy Scouts of America
Brady, James J. 110
Braley, Robert 24
Brassfield erratic 138
Broken Sword, Ohio 60
Bromfield, Louis 112
Browder, Thomas F. 48
Brown, John 16

Brown, Wilson 26
Brown County, Ohio 60
Bruce, Lenny 104
Brunn, Andy 47
Buckeye Lake Cranberry
  Bog 136
Buckeye nickname 114, 116
buckeye tree 114, 116
Buffum, Robert 26, 27
Burns, Richard 24
Butler, Frank 25

Cadiz, Ohio 100, 122
Cain, Emerson 98
Campbell, Mary Cather-
  ine 128
Campbell Hill 113
Canton, Ohio 49, 50, 81,
  97, 147
carbonless copy paper 48
cardinal 114
Carey, Max 47
Case Western Reserve
  University 126
Cash register 48
Casstevens, David 102
Castalia, Ohio 136
Centerburg, Ohio 113
champagne 98
Champaign County, Illi-
  nois 39
Champaign County, Ohio
  39
Champaign County 26, 122
Chapman, John "Johnny
  Appleseed" 146
Chase, Joan 54
Chase, Samuel P. 15
cheese 122
Chesapeake, Ohio 58
chewing gum 97
Chillicothe 118, 121, 129
Christmas 80
Chrostowski, Sharon 110
Cincinnati, Ohio 16, 20,
  21, 22, 23, 24, 29, 31, 39,

48, 49, 50, 55, 67, 86, 87,
  98, 100, 102, 106, 109,
  111, 118, 126, 128, 129,
  131, 133
Cincinnati Arch 38
Cincinnati chili 99
Circleville, Ohio 130
Civil War 15, 71, 75, 83, 88,
  89, 98, 101, 122, 127,
  128, 147
Clark County 138
Clem, Johnny 127
Cleveland, Ohio 16, 18, 19,
  21, 24, 29, 38, 48, 55, 56,
  59, 80, 97, 102, 103, 106,
  108, 110, 122, 123, 126,
  129, 131, 136
Cleveland, Grover 80, 90
Cleveland Playhouse 35
Cleveland Shale 38
Clifton, Ohio 32
Clifton Mill 32
Clinton County 58
Clyde, Ohio 16
Colley, Russell 50
Columbiana, Ohio 62
Columbiana County 59
Columbus, Ohio 24, 25,
  29, 32, 39, 48, 97, 101,
  114, 118, 119, 122, 123,
  124, 126, 127, 128, 129,
  130, 141, 148, 155
Condon, George 55
Congressional Medal of
  Honor 26-29
Conneaut, Ohio 113
Conover, Ohio 50
Constantinople 79
Cooper, Martha Kinney
  129
corn picker 49
Corrigan, Laura 108
Corsica, Ohio 67
Coshocton County 59
Craig, Vernon 148
Crane, Clarence 97

Crawford, Colonel William 60
Creighton, William 119, 121
Crisco 122
Crosley, Powel 50
Cuba, Ohio 58
Curtis, Louise Atcherson 129
Custer, Boston 28
Custer, Gen. George 28, 100
Custer, Luzern 49
Custer, Thomas 28
Cuyahoga Falls, Ohio 50

Danner, Joseph 50
Darke County 16, 64, 130
Davis, Sammy L. 29
Dayton, Ohio 16, 18, 20, 29, 48, 49, 50, 100, 101, 103, 106, 110, 126, 131, 132, 133, 134, 140
Dayton, Ohio 141, 144, 145
Defiance County 26
DeForest, Lee 25
Delaware, Ohio 66, 130, 148
Delightful, Ohio 60
Dennewitz, Mrs. Joseph 129
Denney, Joseph Villiers 100
Dickens, Charles 106
Dickey, Douglas 29
disposable diapers 48
disposable vacuum cleaner bag 48
Do Little or Nothing Machine 49
Donahue, Hessie 129
Dorsey, Daniel 26
Dublin, Ohio 59
Dull, James 62
Dull, Ohio 62
Dunbar, Paul Laurence 16

Duvall, Robert 102

Eaton, General William 62
Eaton, Ohio 62
Ebert, Jacob 122
Eckstein, Gustav 55
Edison, Thomas 16, 49, 50, 101
ejection seat 145
electric dental gold annealer 49
electric light bulb 49
Erie County 136
Estocin, Michael 29
ethyl gasoline 49
Evland, Robert 61
Ewing, Catherine 130

Fairfield County 26, 59
Fall, Albert B. 83
Firsts, Ohio 24-25, 68
Fitzpatrick, Frank 47
Fizzleville, Ohio 60
Fleek, Charles 29
flint 117
flint ridge 137
Florida, Ohio 58
Fly, Ohio 60
Foraker, Joseph 55
Foraker, Julia 55
Ford, Fridelia 124
Ford, Robert 103
Ford, Henry 101
Foster, Charles 127
Franklin County 59, 123
Franklin Township, Ohio 113
Fraze, Ermal 49
Freed, Alan 19
Fulton County 64

Gable, Clark 16, 100, 126
Gahanna, Ohio 117
Gallipolis, Ohio 16, 109
Garfield, Eliza Ballou 84
Garfield, James 60, 66, 70,

71, 74, 79, 87, 88, 90, 94, 96
Gatewood, Emma 109
General Sherman 38
Geneva, Ohio 59
Georgetown, Ohio 122
Gillett, Joel 44
Girl Scout Cookies 99
glacial grooves 137
Glenn, John 123, 127
Gold, William 55
Graham, Dr. Sylvester 122
graham crackers 122
Grant, Julia 86
Grant, Ulysses 15, 66, 69, 71, 73, 75, 77, 87, 88, 89, 90, 94, 96, 122, 128
Gray, John 20, 22, 23
Great Cider Campaign of 18, 40, 76
Great Locomotive Chase 27
Great Seal of Ohio 119, 121
Great Serpent Mound 34
Greenfield, Ohio 48
Greenville, Ohio 29
Grey, Zane 17
Guernsey County 64

Hack, Elsie 123
Hall, Charles Martin 49
Hallock, Robert Lay 48
Hamburger 97
Hamilton, Margaret 16
Hamilton County 138
Hancock County 26
*Hang on Sloopy* 117
Harding, Florence Kling DeWolfe 86
Harding, Warren Gamaliel 67, 68, 69, 70, 71, 72, 73, 75, 82, 83, 88, 90, 91, 96, 129
Harlow, Alvin 55, 56
Harris, Harold L. 144
Harrison, Anna Symmes 84, 86
Harrison, Benjamin 67, 70, 71, 74, 75, 76, 80, 84, 88, 89, 90, 94, 96, 127
Harrison, Caroline Scott 80, 85
Harrison, John Scott 84
Harrison, William Henry 19, 66, 69, 76, 80, 84, 86, 87, 88, 90, 91, 94, 96, 116
Hatcher, Harlan 56
Havighurst, Walter 56
Hawaii 77
Hawkins, Martin 26
Hayes, Lucy Webb 68, 85
Hayes, Rutherford B. 66, 71, 78, 88, 89, 90, 96
Hearst, William Randolph 19
Hebrew Union College 131
Henry 50
Henry County 58
Herda, Frank 29
Hiett, Ohio 60
Highland County 57, 58, 138
Hiramsburg, Ohio 20
Holden, William 103
Holmes County 59
Homer, Ohio 132
hot dog 97
Hughes, Lloyd 49
Hussey, Obed 50

*I Want To Go To Morrow* 63
Indians 21, 24, 34, 88, 100, 118, 127, 130, 138
Ingalls Building 24
Isle St. George 35
Ivory soap 49

Jackson, Ohio 63
Jakes, John 103
Janek, Gregory 50
Jefferson County 26, 59

Johnny Marzetti 97
Johnson, Josephine 56
Jones, Tom 146

Kalakaua, David 77
Karam, Adib 109
Kaye, Danny 102
Kelleys Island 137
Kellogg, Dr. J. 71
Kent State University 110
Kenyon College 96
Kettering, Charles 48, 101,
    109, 144
King, Robert 115
Kipling, Ohio 64
Kiradjieff, Athanas 99
Kirk, Steve 110
Kitchen, Tella 16
Knight, William 26
Knockemstiff, Ohio 61
Knox County 128

ladybug 117
Lake County 10, 113
Lake Erie 113, 138
Lambert, Larry 145
Lambert, John 49
Lancaster, Ohio 16, 19, 38,
    101
LaPointe, Joseph 29
Lasts, Ohio 20-23
Lawrence County, Ohio 58
Lazarus Department
    Stores 24
Lebanon, Ohio 45
Lee, Robert E. 71
LeMay, Gen. Curtis 127
Li, Tien 49
Licking County 136, 137
life saver candy 97
life saving net 48
lightning "bug" 144
Lima, Ohio 58, 104
Lincoln, Abraham 75, 100
Lindbergh, Charles 144
Lisbon, Ohio 59

Livingston, Alexander 46
Logan County 26
London, Ohio 58
Longworth, Nicholas 98
Longworth, Alice Roose-
    velt 73
Lucas County 124

MacGahan, J.S. 127
Madison, Ohio 63
Madison County 58
mammoths 137
Mann, Horace 127
Mantua, Ohio 58
manure spreader 49
Marietta, Ohio 116, 118,
    130
Marietta College 139
Marion, Ohio 86
Martha (passenger pi-
    geon) 21-23
Martin, Delia Corbly 146
Martin, Dean 16
Marzetti, Mary 97
Mason, Elihu 26, 27
Massillon, Ohio 126
mastodons 137
Mastronardo, James 115
Matthews, Jack 57
Matz, James 109
Maugins, Dwight 146
McAdoo, William 91
McCabe, Harriet Clark 130
McElroy Minster Com-
    pany 25
McGuffey Lane 38
McGuffey Reader 31
McIntyre, O.O. 16
McKinley, William 15, 38,
    67, 71, 81, 87, 88, 89, 90,
    91, 92, 95, 96, 147
McKloskey, W.H. 47
McVicker, Joseph 49
Medina, Ohio 45
Medina County 64
Meeker, Ezra 108

Menches, Frank 97
menthol cigarette 49
Mercer County 47, 49
meteorites 138
Mettle, Eric 47
Mexico 89
Miami County 61, 146
Miami University 31, 96, 127
Miamisburg, Ohio 110, 122, 123
Middletown, Ohio 29
Midgely, Thomas 49
Milan, Ohio 16, 49, 101
Milligan, William 148
Mills, Fanny 147, 149
Mingo Junction, Ohio 49
Miscavich, William 49
Mitchell, Dwight 110
Mitchell, Tom 47
Mock, Jerrie 39, 130
money 15
Monroe County, Ohio 60
Montgomery County 138
Morgan, Garrett 48
Morrow, Jeremiah 62
Morrow, Ohio 62
Moscow, Ohio 59
Moses, Edwin 20
Motto, Frank 128
Mt. Beard 39
Mt. Logan 119
Mt. McKinley 38, 39
Mt. Vernon 97
Mullins Manufacturing 40
Murray, Jim 104
Muskingum County 24, 26, 137

Napoleon, Prince 106
NCR Corporation 48
Nels, Al 39
Nelson, Martha 34
New Concord, Ohio 123, 126, 138
New Concord Meteorite
139
New Jersey 38
New Lexington, Ohio 127
New Rumley, Ohio 28, 100
Newark, Ohio 48, 147
Newlin, Melvin 29
Newman, Steve 111
Niles, Ohio 67, 97
Nissenson, Hugh 103
Noble County 24, 113
Non-Hel-E-Ma 130
North Bend, Ohio 24, 66, 67, 84
North Central Great Lakes Region 117
Northwest Territory 19, 88, 118

O'Hara, Scarlett 103
Oakley, Annie 127, 130
Oberlin, Ohio 49, 131, 132
Oberlin College 122
Ochs, Adolph S. 100
Ohio, origin of word 118
Ohio River 58
Ohio Central College 96
Ohio lemon pie 99
Ohio State Fair 99, 123
Ohio State University 32, 46, 100, 127
Ohio Statehood 118
Ohio Statehouse 118, 119, 120-121
Ohio University 35
Ohioana Library Association 129
Ohlin, Mark and Randy 47
Oldfield, Berna Eli "Barney" 25
Oppenheim, Mrs. Joseph 49
Orange, Ohio 66
Oregonia, Ohio 138
Orick, Abner 100
Orr, Noah 147

Outcault, Richard 19
Oxford, Ohio 31

parachute 144
Paraguay 79
Paris, Ohio 59
Parmalee, Philip 141
Parrott, Jacob 26, 27
passenger pigeons 21
Patrick, Peter 61
Paul, Joe 29
Long, Donal 29
Pee Pee, Ohio 61
Perry, Oliver Hazard 100
Perry County 100
Perrysville, Ohio 108
Peters, Mike 106
Pflueger, Ernest 48
Philadelphia, PA 75
Phoneton, Ohio 61
Pike County 26, 61
Pittenger, William 26, 27
Pittsburgh, Pennsylvania 38, 83
Play-Doh 49
poetry day 117
Point Pleasant, Ohio 66, 130
Poland, Ohio 47
Poland China Hog 45
Pomeroy, Ohio 126
Poole, C.A. 47
pop-top can 49
Portage County 26, 47, 58
Porter, John 26
Porter, Sherwin 122
Portsmouth, Ohio 47, 127
Portsmouth Shale 39
potato chips 98
Preble, Capt. Edward 62
Preble County 62, 138
Preparation H 50
Presidents, U.S. 65-96
Price, Issac 47
Pricetown, Ohio 138
Priesand, Sally Jane 131

Procter & Gamble 24, 31, 48, 49, 111
Proctorville, Ohio 44
Ptolemy I 15
Pulitzer, Joseph 19

Quaker Oats 98
Queen Victoria 78, 130, 147

R.G. Barry Company 25
Rader, E.J. 24
Raffington, Matthew G. 48
Rankin, John 104
Rawlinson, Gordon 19
reaper 50
Records, Ohio 70
red carnation 114
Reddick, William H. 26, 27
Resnick, Judith 131
revolving bookcase 50
Richter, Conrad 56
Riley, Capt. James 62
Riley, James Whitcomb 104
Ripley, Ohio 104
Ritty, James S. 48
River Styx 64
Roberts, Gordon 29
Robertson, Samuel 26
Rogers, Roy 127
roller bearing 50
Rome, Ohio 59
Rome Beauty Apple 44
Roosevelt, Theodore 82, 95
Root, Amos Ives 44, 45
Ross, Marion 26
Ross County 16, 34, 61
Russia, Ohio 59

salt 138
Salter, Susanna Madora 131
San Francisco, CA 78, 110
Sanders, Scott 57
Sandusky, Ohio 99, 147, 149

Santmyer, Helen Hooven 57
Savannah, Ohio 49
Schee, Dougie and Debbie 148
Scherer, Pete 47
Schraidt, Caspar 99
Schroeder, Rudolph "Shorty" 144, 145
Schumacher, Ferdinand 98
Schwarz, Jo and Hermene 131
Scioto County 26, 39
Semple, William F. 97
Sequoia National Park, California 38
Sessions, Lucy 131
Seville, Ohio 147
Shakers 45, 46, 99
Shawnee, Mars 39
Shawnee, Ohio 39
Shelby County 47, 136
Shelvador 50
Sheridan, Gen. Philip 100
Sherman, John 18
Sherman, Gen. William Tecumseh 16, 38, 101, 127, 128
Shriver, H.B. 49
Shutt, Paul 49
Sidney, Ohio 47
Slavens, Samuel 26
Smart, Charles Allen 57
Smith, Floyd 144
Smith, Jedediah Strong 108
Snyder, Laurence H. 127
soda fountain 122
Sodom, Ohio 64
South Olive, Ohio 24
South Point, Ohio 113
Space suit 50
Spaghetti fork 49
Spangler, Murray 50
Spellacy, William 59
Sperti, George 50

Spirit of Columbus 3
Spirit of Dayton 39
Spofford, Fisher A. 48
Sproat, Col. Ebenezer 116
Stanton, Edwin M. 100
Stark County 59
State of Ohio motto, nickname, tree, etc. 114-117, 126
Steffens, Lincoln 106
Steinem, Gloria 131
stepladder 50
Steubenville, Ohio 16
Steuk Wine Company 99
Stevens, Harry M. 97
Stone, Lucy 132
Story, Nelson 24
Sullivan, Tim 103
Symmes, John Cleves 86

Taft, Helen 85, 95
Taft, William Howard 67, 70, 71, 75, 82, 86, 87, 88, 90, 91, 95, 96
TAT Restaurant
Taylor, Bayard 106
Taylor, Carl Rutherford 123
Tecumseh 100, 127
Tewart, Bonnie 46
Texas, Ohio 58
Thacker, Brian 29
Thomas, Lowell 16
Thompson, Parke 110
Thompson, Thelva 47
Thurber, James 57
Tilden, Samuel 90
Timken, Henry 50
toilet seat 50
Toledo, Ohio 25, 104
tomato juice 117
tomatoes 46
train robbery, first 25
Treaty of Greenville 21
Trillium grandiflorum 117
trilobite 117
Trollope, Frances 102

Troy, Ohio 25
Trumbull, Ohio 64
Trumbull County 60

*U.S. Akron* 30, 38
*U.S.S. Cincinnati* 40
*U.S.S. Cleveland* 40
*U.S.S. Columbus* 40
*U.S.S. Dayton* 40
*U.S.S. Lansdowne* 39
*U.S.S. Lorain County* 40
*U.S.S. Ohio* 40
*U.S.S. Pickaway* 40
*U.S.S. Shenandoah* 39, 41
Union City, Ohio 104
Union County 147
United States Congress
    15, 18, 27, 80, 84, 85, 120
United States Supreme
    Court 82
United States Treasury 15
University of Alabama 83
University of Cincinnati 34
Urbana, Illinois 39
Urbana, Ohio 39
Urichsville, Ohio 126

vacuum cleaner 50
Van Wert County 62
VFW (Veterans of Foreign
    Wars) 24
Virginia 66

Wagner's Potato Chips
    123
Wallace, Lew 79
Walton, George 44
Wapakoneta, Ohio 101, 108
War of 1812 88, 100
Warner, Albert, Jack,
    Harry, and Sam 17
Warren, Ohio 40
Warren County 45, 62
Warsaw, Ohio 59
Washington, Ohio 63
Washington, D.C. 75, 76,
    85, 94, 95, 110, 120, 128,

133, 134
Washington County 113
Wauseon, Ohio 25
Wayne, Ohio 46
Wayne County 26, 138
Wellsville, Ohio 29
Wendy's restaurants 124
Westlake, Ohio 19
White, William Allen 91
White, Curtis 110
White House 75, 78, 80,
    82, 83, 84, 85, 95, 123,
    127
white tail deer 117
Willshire, Ohio 62
Willshire, William 62
Wilmington, Ohio 110
Wilson, John 26
Winder, David 29
wine 98, 99
Winton, Alexander 18
Wittenmeier, Rudy 123
Wood, Mark 26
Wood County 26
Woodhull, Victoria Claflin
    77, 132
Wooster, Ohio 46, 148
words, with Ohio origins
    18, 19, 68, 69
World War I 73
Worthington, Thomas 121
Wright, Katharine 132, 140
Wright, Orville 16, 101, 103,
    132, 140, 141
Wright, Wilbur 16, 101, 103,
    132, 140, 141
Wright-Patterson Air Force
    Base 18

Xenia, Ohio 57

Yellow Springs, Ohio 104
Youngstown, Ohio 17

Zanesville, Ohio 17, 118,
    126
Zeta Beta Tau 123